SUPERNATURAL VANISHINGS

Otherworldly Disappearances

Rodney Davies

Sterling Publishing Co., Inc. New York

Yes, you are quite right, we are describing an
impossible phenomenon; and yet it is true!
Professor Charles Richet

Library of Congress Cataloging-in-Publication Data Available

10   9   8   7   6   5   4   3   2   1

Published 1996 by Sterling Publishing Company, Inc.
387 Park Avenue South, New York, N.Y. 10016
Originally published 1995 in Great Britain by
Robert Hale Limited under the title *Supernatural Disappearances*
© 1995 by Rodney Davies
Distributed in Canada by Sterling Publishing
% Canadian Manda Group, One Atlantic Avenue, Suite 105
Toronto, Ontario, Canada M6K 3E7
Manufactured in the United States of America

Sterling ISBN 0-8069-4896-5

Contents

Acknowledgements   7
Introduction   9

  1   Some Classical Disappearances   13
  2   Devilish Movements   25
  3   Mysterious Appearances   39
  4   Bilocation   59
  5   Animal Entrances and Exits   77
  6   Slipping Away in Somerset   83
  7   Benjamin Bathurst's Trousers   95
  8   Going, Going, Gone   113
  9   Can Such Things Really Be?   129
10   Vanishing Ships and Aircraft   145
11   The Medium is the Message   159
12   Comments and Conclusions   173

Index   181

To all those who have vanished
without trace.

Acknowledgements

The writing of this book, perhaps not surprisingly, has occasioned a great deal of research. This has been a largely enjoyable task, yet one fraught with difficulty, as many of the references I initially obtained proved to be inaccurate, giving as they variously did wrong names, wrong places, wrong dates and wrong details. To obtain accurate information I have gone where possible to the original source, but when not, I have taken the balance of opinion. My wholehearted thanks go to the following institutions and their staff: the British Library, the Newspaper Library at Colindale, the Barnet Libraries, particularly my local library at Church End, Finchley, and of course to the stalwart British taxpayer, who finances their maintenance and operation.

My gratitude also goes to the Redfern Library at McGill University, Montreal, and to John and Joyce Matthews of the Two Jays Bookshop at Edgware for finding me several books that would otherwise have been unobtainable. Lastly, I would like to thank again those individuals, mentioned in the text, who replied to my queries about a supernatural disappearance which supposedly took place in their particular locality.

The copyright material shown below is kindly reprinted by permission of the publishers.

Philostratus: *The Life of Apollonius*, Volume 16, translated by F.C. Conybeare, Loeb Classical Library, Cambridge, Mass., Harvard University Press (1965); Wellesley Tudor Pole: *The Silent Road*, Neville Spearman Publishers, imprint of the C.W. Daniel Company Limited (1972); *The SPR Newsletter*, The Society for Psychical Research (1987); Kate Norgate: *William of Newburgh*, The Dictionary of National Biography, Oxford University Press; Gwendolen Kelley Hack: *Modern Mysteries at Millesimo Castle*,

Rider & Co (1956); Alexandra David-Neel: *Magic and Mystery in Tibet*, Unwin Paperbacks, imprint of the Souvenir Press (1965); Uri Geller: *My Story*, Robson Books Limited (1976).

Introduction

The principal characteristics that I remember about the woman who unwittingly inspired this book, in the short span of time that I saw her, were the black and white polka dot dress that she wore and the toy dog that walked beside her on a lead she held in her right hand. I also have a somewhat less precise recollection of her brown hair, which was curled up from the hairline, as if mimicking a wave that was poised to fall, in a conventional early 1950s style, on to the crown of her head. She was probably in her mid-thirties, although it is very hard to accurately estimate the age of an adult when you are only ten years old, as I then was. But she was certainly not an old woman, and she walked down the narrow path towards my friend and me at a brisk and lively pace. She seemed intent on giving her small companion some good exercise.

We, John and I, were hurrying back to the Devon holiday camp where we had met, and become friends, one week earlier, and where we had since enjoyed each other's company. It was now the day of our departure, and we had spent the morning making a last and regretful visit to a nearby reservoir, which was reached by taking this path bordered on both sides by a tall hedge, and where we had thrown flat stones edgewise at the water's glistening and inviting surface, to make them bounce and skip across it. It was the final escapade of a happy week, before our parents took us back to our respective ordinary worlds.

But for me, the woman with the Yorkshire terrier changed that last sunny, carefree outing into a completely unexpected and unforgettable morning of terror. For when she was about twenty yards away, she suddenly turned to her right and left the path through what I presumed was a gap in the hedge, to enter, or so it seemed, the adjacent pasture field. Yet when we reached the spot where she had turned off, I found to my surprise that not only was

9

there no gap in the hedge, but neither was there any sign of her or her dog in the field. The woman in the polka dot dress and her undersized canine had literally disappeared!

I gasped in astonishment and turned to John, who was behind me. 'What,' I cried out to him, 'happened to her?'

He frowned, puzzled. 'What happened to who?'

'To the woman with the dog who came down the path.'

'I didn't see a woman,' John insisted, looking quickly about him. 'Or a dog.'

'But you must have,' I said, feeling my skin grow cold. 'She – she was wearing a polka dot dress. I thought she went through a gap in the hedge here, except there isn't one, is there?'

'No,' said John, his eyes now wide and staring.

'She just vanished!' I gasped, suddenly more frightened than I had ever been.

'Oh God!' murmured John, picking up on my fear, his face whitening.

'Let's go!' I shouted and began running. John followed my example, and we carried on running, fast and scared, until we were safely back at the holiday camp with our parents, although mine, after castigating me for being late, listened to my tale of terror with studied adult nonchalance. I had obviously, they concluded, been mistaken about the position of the gap in the hedge. That must be the explanation, for everybody knows that people, or dogs for that matter, can't just vanish into thin air. Such things are simply impossible!

Prompted by such a parental put-down, yet needing to explain what had happened, I thought for a long time afterwards that maybe I had seen a ghost, or rather two ghosts, on that morning, whereas later, when I found out about such things, I wondered if I had had an hallucination. Both possibilities were supported by the fact that John had seen nothing unusual, although he had been behind me, with the way ahead partly obscured by my body, while his attention might easily have been caught by something on the ground or at the path's side to make him miss seeing the woman and her dog in the minute or two that they were visible to me. But I knew deep down that there had been nothing ghostly about the figures, no haziness of form or oddness of appearance, to suggest they were not of this world. Indeed, the woman's polka dot dress and hairstyle had been unremarkably real and up to date. And I came to conclude that her and her dog's existence as hallucinations seemed as unlikely as my seeing a mirage in the Devon landscape. After all, if they were spontaneous products of my mind, why should I have seen such figures only once in my life and at that particular moment?

That left two explanations: the first and common-sense one taken by my parents, that I was mistaken in my perception of what had happened to the woman and her dog, that she really went through a gap in the hedge, which I must have missed, just as I somehow missed seeing her in the field; and the second, which I felt in my heart to be true despite all protestations by others, that she and her Yorkie had really vanished.

The very idea of the latter alternative, by which I mean the supernatural disappearance of a person, animal or non-living object in front of witnesses, or in circumstances that make another explanation untenable, is regarded by most people as completely impossible. Indeed, it is so at odds with our everyday experience of what we like to call reality, that practically everyone, at least in our scientific culture, would vehemently deny that it ever happens.

Yet none the less, when it is understood that the human body, like everything else in the universe, consists of far more empty space than matter, to the extent that if the atoms giving it the semblance of substance were compressed together until they touched one another, it – that is, yourself or myself – could easily pass through the eye of a needle, our apparent solidity becomes a will-o'-the-wisp. In fact the wonder of it all is not, as the cases recorded in this book make plain, that material objects sometimes do supernaturally disappear, but that they do not vanish from sight far more often.

As we shall see, those who disappear in this strange manner may never return, while others may reappear, seemingly instantly, at a distant location. And because the latter manifestation may be observed by witnesses when the former is not, such supernatural appearances are also described in this book as part of the overall record. So too are those instances of bilocation, the most incredible phenomenon of all, whereby the body of the person concerned is supernaturally duplicated, the double sometimes appearing at a distant place. Hardly surprisingly, bilocation happens most frequently to saints and to other holy men and women.

All these occurrences, while of course rare and unusual, have a long history, which is why I have written about both ancient and modern instances. For although any one case may be airily dismissed as the product of faulty observation, of simple error, or even of fraud, by the sceptic, when taken together they constitute sufficient proof that we do not live in a totally closed and orderly world, wherein events that defy rationality cannot occur. Rather, they reveal that the unexpected and the miraculous can and still do happen, and that the realm of wonder, magic and fairy is still very much with us and around us.

R.D., Finchley, England.

1 Some Classical Disappearances

But Aphrodite used her powers once more. Hiding Paris in a
dense mist, she whisked him off – it was an easy feat for the
goddess – and put him down in his own perfumed fragrant
bedroom.

From the *Iliad*, Book III by Homer

The phenomenon of the supernatural disappearance is recorded in
the earliest written works. Several examples of it are mentioned by
the Greek poet Homer in his *Iliad*, which was composed in the
eighth century BC, and the Old Testament provides us with more,
notably the miraculous departures from the world of the patriarch
Enoch and the prophet Elijah.

But I will begin by looking at some slightly later supernatural
disappearances, starting at the borderline period where myth rubs
shoulders with history, and then moving on to classical times,
although all the cases examined, while not widely known, are
classics of their kind. It will enable you to take note of their
distinguishing features, which may provide clues as to why and
how they occur.

The first disappearance I shall consider happened to a Roman,
in fact to the first Roman, for the person who mysteriously
vanished is none other than Romulus, from whom the name of
Rome derives. Romulus founded Rome with his twin brother
Remus in 753 BC, became king of the city later that same year, and
went on to rule it for the following thirty-nine years.

Romulus and Remus are popularly regarded as legendary
figures, yet there is no good reason to think that they did not exist.
Their so-called divine birth – they were said to be the sons of the
war god Mars – was one frequently claimed by, or for, many

famous men and women of the ancient world, and the tale of their suckling by a she-wolf originates from their wet-nurse, who was a prostitute nicknamed Lupus or 'Wolf'. In fact the strength of the tradition surrounding them unequivocably marks them out as real personages.

There are several accounts of Romulus's disappearance, all slightly different. One version has him inexplicably vanishing while giving instructions to Rome's senators at the temple of Vulcan on the afternoon of 7 July 714 BC. Yet because a sudden darkness accompanied the event, it is more likely that his mysterious exit from the world happened on 26 May of that year, when there was an eclipse of the sun, although the inaccuracy of the Roman calendar at that time could easily account for the discrepancy between the dates.

However, the Roman author Livius Titus or Livy, writing of Romulus's disappearance in his *The Early History of Rome*, describes it thus: 'One day while he was reviewing his troops on the Campus Martius near the marsh of Capra, a storm burst, with violent thunder. A cloud enveloped him, so thick that it hid him from the eyes of everyone present; and from that moment he was never seen again upon earth.'

Livy's account, differing in location – the 'marsh of Capra' or Goats' Marsh lay outside Rome – and the occasion, a review of troops as opposed to a meeting with senators, includes the detail of Romulus's being obscured by a thick cloud rather than a darkness prior to his miraculous departure.

Another version, given by the Greek writer Plutarch, also has him vanishing at Goats' Marsh, apparently during an assembly held there which was attended by both senators and citizens. Plutarch says:

the air on that occasion was suddenly convulsed and altered in a wonderful manner; for the light of the sun failed and they were involved in an astonishing darkness, attended on every side with dreadful thunderings and tempestuous winds. The multitude then dispersed and fled, but the nobility gathered into one body. When the tempest was over, and the light appeared again, the people returned to the same place, and a very anxious enquiry was made for the king – but without him being found.

Plutarch's version represents Romulus's disappearance as being accompanied by both an eclipse and by the violent storm mentioned by Livy, which would certainly have made a frightening combination and prompted people to run for their lives. And as we shall discover, one or other of these dramatic meteorological happenings has occurred at some later disappearances.

Because the search for Romulus failed to locate either him or even one fragment of his clothing, murmurings began among the people that the senators had murdered him and had cut his body and clothing into small pieces, which they had then separately removed, hidden under their own clothes, to remote and out-of-the-way places. Yet while such a deep hatred for Romulus may well have existed among those senators who were jealous of him or tired of his rule, it seems quite implausible that they could have disposed of his corpse by dissection, in such a limited time, without giving themselves away by the large quantity of blood that would have been shed, or by the accompanying dreadful mess that would have been made. It is also unlikely that none of these men, if they had committed such an appalling crime, inadvertently told their wives or mistresses what they had done or later confessed to it on their deathbeds. But there are no reports of such a confession or slip of the tongue by any of them. This alone points to their innocence.

However, all such speculation was soon put to an end by an elderly and distinguished senator named Julius Proculus, who was renowned for his sanctity and who claimed under oath to have met Romulus on the road outside Rome while returning to the city, 'in a form more noble and august than ever, and clad in bright and dazzling armour'. The reconstituted Romulus, whose return is reminiscent of the supernatural reappearance of Jesus Christ at Emmaus, told the old senator:

> It pleases the gods, my good Proculus, that we should dwell with men for a time; and after having founded a city which will be the most powerful and glorious in the world, return to heaven, from whence we came. Farewell then, and go, tell the Romans, that, by the exercise of temperance and fortitude, they shall attain the highest pitch of human greatness; and I the god Quirinus will ever be propitious to you.

By this speech Romulus confirmed his divinity (which derived from his 'father' Mars) and revealed that he had become the god Quirinus. As such he was worshipped at Rome for the next thousand years.

The second supernatural disappearance which we know about in some detail, and which is a very remarkable one, gains credence from the fact that it did not happen to a hero or to a king, but instead to an ordinary citizen.

It took place on an island named Proconnesus situated in the Sea of Marmara, which the ancients called the Propontis, in about the year 550 BC. The man who vanished was named Aristeas, and he later became a celebrated poet.

Proconnesus, which was alternatively known as Elaphonnesus or Neuris, is today called Marmara. It lies to the north-west of, and about six miles from, a large promontory named Kapidagi Yarimadasi (see Figure 1), but which was then an island called Cyzicum (or Arctonnesus). Both islands were settled by the

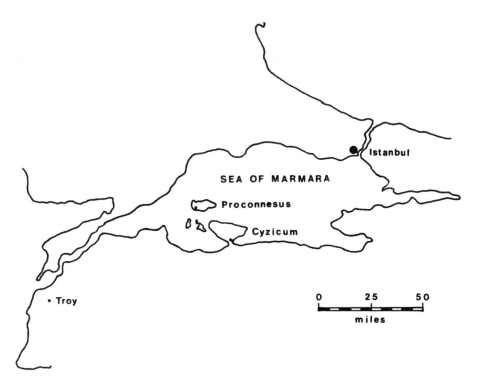

Figure 1   Position of the island of Proconnesus

Greeks, probably in the mid-eighth century BC. Cyzicum was named after Cyzicus, one of the Argonauts, who was accidentally killed there by Jason, their leader, when they stopped at the island *en route* for Colchis and were attacked in the night by its savage inhabitants.

Apparently one day Aristeas, who was only a young man and a budding poet at the time, visited a wool cleanser's or fuller's shop in the main town (also called Proconnesus) where he lived. While in conversation with the shop's owner Aristeas suddenly cried out and fell to the ground, and it was quickly determined by the startled owner that he was dead. The man hurriedly locked up his shop and went off to tell Aristeas's relatives of the tragedy, yet when he returned with them and re-entered the shop, all were staggered to find that it was empty. Aristeas's body had literally vanished, a fact that was vouched for by neighbouring retailers who said that no one had left the shop or entered it since the owner had locked it and departed.

But something reminiscent of Romulus's disappearance was to follow, for not long afterwards a man arrived from Cyzicus, the chief town and port of Cyzicum, to say that while he was travelling into the town from the nearby seaport of Artaca, which he had been visiting, he had met Aristeas on the road and had stopped to talk with him. Hence the missing dead man had not only supernaturally disappeared, but had reappeared several miles away, on another island, alive again!

The Greek historian Herodotus claims that seven years later Aristeas returned, quite unannounced, to Proconnesus, where he remained long enough to compose a long poem entitled *The Tale of the Arimaspians*. This was apparently based on the visits he had made to various barbarian tribes during his absence, most notably a Scythian tribe called the Issedones, who lived to the north-east of the Caspian Sea. They had told him of the Arimaspi, who lived, they said, some distance beyond them and who were unique in being mono-ocular, or one-eyed. These improbable people were engaged in constant warfare with an even more improbable group, the griffins, who dwelt beyond them, deep in the vast coniferous forests of the region, and who guarded large deposits of gold.

When Aristeas completed *The Tale of the Arimaspians* he disappeared again (although not apparently supernaturally) and never returned to his native island. However, this was not entirely the last that was heard of him, as 240 years later his ghost manifested at the town of Metapontum in southern Italy, where it spoke to those who witnessed it and told them to erect a statue of him near to the temple of Apollo. His instructions were carried out and the town subsequently prospered. But regretfully, the years have not treated his poem so kindly, and it has been, with the exception of a few verses quoted by other authors, entirely lost. And to this day the gold of the griffins, if it ever existed, remains undiscovered.

Interestingly, the philosopher Pythagoras spent the last years of his life in Metapontum, a coastal town situated on the instep of the Italian boot, dying there *c.* 497 BC. It was from Metapontum that on one occasion he reputedly supernaturally transported himself (by uttering magic words) to Taurominium in Sicily, a distance of almost 300 miles by sea, which enabled him to speak with friends in both towns on the same day, something that would ordinarily have been quite impossible for him to do. Yet so many wonderful tales are told about Pythagoras, who achieved universal fame during his lifetime through his philosophical and mathematical discoveries and his teachings, that it is difficult to know which of them, if any, are true.

The next well-documented and famous disappearance I would like to consider also took place on an island, named Astypalea, which lies between Cos and Carpathos, in the Aegean Sea (see Figure 2). The person who vanished was Cleomedes, a famous boxer of his day, who represented Astypalea at the Olympic Games in either 496 or 492 BC.

Cleomedes was a very large and powerful man, and was the natural favourite to win the boxing event. He in fact reached the final without too much trouble, but his opponent, Iccus from Epidaurus, was also a fine, strong boxer, who evidently gave Cleomedes a much tougher time of it than he had expected. This led the impetuous Cleomedes to throw a foul punch, with which he accidentally killed poor Iccus. The umpires then disqualified Cleomedes, the shock of which, along with that caused by the death of his opponent, unsettled his brain.

The disgraced and bitter boxer returned to Astypalea, not to a hero's welcome, but to the taunts and recriminations of his fellow islanders, who had expected so much of him. Cleomedes's mind snapped completely, and not long afterwards he entered a school

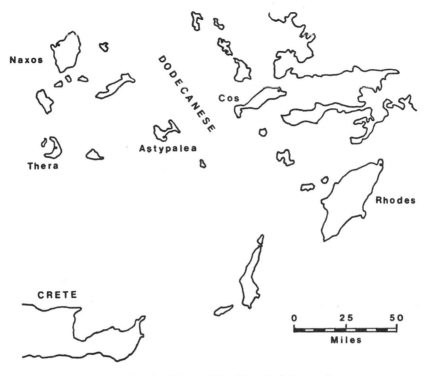

Figure 2 Position of the island of Astypalea

and either struck down, or pulled down, a pillar supporting the roof, which collapsed on to the pupils and killed about sixty of them. It wasn't long before the grief-stricken and enraged parents went looking for Cleomedes, intending to stone him to death. The badly frightened boxer ran off and took sanctuary in the temple of Athene, where, as an extra safeguard, he shut himself in a large strongbox or chest, whose lid he held down so tightly that the angry parents found that they could not pull it open. Axes were sent for, and it wasn't long before the chest was hacked to pieces. But to everybody's surprise, it was found to be empty. Cleomedes had vanished into thin air!

The islanders, realizing that they had witnessed a miracle, hurriedly sent a party to the Delphic oracle to enquire as to what it could mean. The answer they received came as another shock, for the priestess, the Pythia, told them in her trance: '*Ultimus heroum Cleomedes Astypalaeus* – The race of heroes ends with Cleomedes of Astypalea.' This led the Astypaleans to worship Cleomedes as a demigod, his cult being continued among them for about 650 years.

In 217 BC, more than 250 years after the supernatural disappearance of Cleomedes, an important battle took place in Italy between the Romans and the Carthaginian army led by Hannibal, near Lake Thrasymenus in Tuscany, which resulted in the unaccountable disappearance of the Roman commander, Caius Flaminius.

Caius Flaminius was a consul, a man of a fiery and headstrong personality, whose successes in earlier battles had made him foolishly over-confident of victory. He even ignored a number of negative omens which might have warned him of coming peril. For example, his horse suddenly took fright one day for no apparent reason, throwing him from its back, yet he refused to accept that the accident might presage his own downfall.

The Roman army had the advantage in numbers, and Hannibal, realizing this, prepared to defeat them by means of strategy. He therefore lured them into an ambush between the lake and the nearby Corona hills, where the two advantages of surprise and geography enabled him to cut them to pieces. Indeed, the battle of Lake Thrasymenus was one of the worst disasters in Roman history, with 15,000 Romans being slaughtered, compared to only 1,500 Carthaginians, and 10,000 being taken prisoner.

Among the Roman dead was their commander, Caius Flaminius, who had fought bravely to the end. In fact Hannibal, who had witnessed his death, was so impressed with his courage that he decided to have him buried with full military honours. He therefore immediately sent to have his body brought from the battlefield. Yet despite a most careful and thorough search being made, Caius Flaminius's corpse was never found. Neither was he, nor could he have been, carried from the battlefield by the fleeing and wounded Romans, as their accounts make plain that he was not seen by them after the battle. The remains of that brave, but foolhardy soldier, had seemingly gone, along with his soul, to 'the undiscovered country from whose bourn no traveller returns'.

The Roman world also provides us with the strange story of the historian Drusus Caius, who when he was a baby was one day found to be missing from his cradle. A search was made for him without success, his increasingly frantic parents coming to the conclusion that someone must have absconded with him. Yet on the following day, quite by chance, the helpless infant was discovered lying near a window in the uppermost part of the house, safe and well, and happily engaged in looking at the sunshine!

Another classical figure who is credited with disappearing before witnesses and appearing within the same hour at a distant place is the famous thaumaturge or 'miracle-worker' Apollonius of Tyana. In fact Apollonius's life is so full of acts of goodness, philosophical enquiry, and reputed marvels, that had he been a Christian he would certainly have been made a saint.

Tyana was an old colonial Greek city situated at the foot of the Taurus mountains in the Roman province of Cappadocia (now south-eastern Turkey), and Apollonius's birth there was attended by certain portents which presaged his future greatness. He became interested in philosophy as a teenager, studied the teachings of several masters, and eventually became a disciple of Pythagoras. At the age of twenty, following his father's death, he began five years of mystic silence, during which the secret truths of Pythagoras were revealed to him. He then embarked upon a series of extensive travels that took him to such faraway places as the Middle East, India, Ethiopia, Egypt, Greece, and Italy, which not only brought him into contact with famous thinkers and with those skilled in magic and other occult arts, from whom he learned much, but which enabled him to develop his own supernatural powers. He soon became known, like Jesus, as a healer, a raiser of the dead, a prophet, and also a divine legislator. Remarkably, he had the ability to understand every foreign language. He adopted a number of personal habits that were eccentric for their time, but which seem now surprisingly modern. He ate no meat, wore no skins, furs or other animal products, and refused to harm or sacrifice animals. He likewise never shaved or cut his hair.

His life was first recorded by his disciple Damis, whose journal, along with other writings about him, was used by Flavius Philostratus, at the command of the emperor Septimius Severus's wife Julia Domna, to compose his famous *The Life of Apollonius of Tyana* about one hundred years after his death. Philostratus says that Apollonius supernaturally disappeared and was teleported to a distant place on two occasions.

The first occasion happened shortly after the sage's return from India (the exact date is uncertain), when he was visiting the Ionian port of Smyrna, 'but when the plague began to rage at Ephesus, and no remedy sufficed to check it, they sent a deputation to Apollonius, asking him to become physician of their infirmity'. Apollonius had already foreseen that Ephesus (about thirty-five miles away) would suffer the outbreak, and understanding its severity 'he thought that he ought not to postpone his journey, but said, "Let us go." And forthwith he was in Ephesus, performing the same feat, I believe, as Pythagoras, who was at Thurii [sic] and Metapontum at one and the same moment'. There he managed to identify the cause of the plague, a demon disguised as an old beggar, and have it destroyed. In this way he stopped the infection.

The second occurrence took place in the year AD 81, when Apollonius was summoned to Rome to appear before the new emperor Domitian to answer charges that he had plotted against him. He was also accused of having sacrificed a boy to divine the future and of allowing himself to be worshipped as a god.

Apollonius was then a venerable old man, yet he defended himself skilfully in court, winning applause from all those present, and obliging Domitian to acquit him of the charges, but saying that the sage must remain in Rome for the time being as he wished to speak to him privately. Apollonius thanked the Emperor, warned him of the trouble that his own accusers were causing others like himself, and quoted a line from Homer: 'For thou shalt not slay me, since I tell thee I am not mortal.'

> And with these words [continues Philostratus], he vanished from the court, which was the best thing that he could do in the circumstances, for the Emperor clearly intended not to question him sincerely about the case, but about all sorts of irrelevant matters ... the effect upon the despot of his quitting the court in a manner so godlike and inexplicable was quite other than that which the many expected; for they expected him to make a terrific uproar and institute a hunt for the man, and send forth proclamations over his empire to arrest him wherever they should find him. But he did nothing of the kind.

Apollonius's disappearance from the crowded court-room took place at about noon. At dusk of the same day he surprised his disciples Damis and Demetrius by appearing to them in a distant temple built to the nymphs, which stood on a beach near to the town of Dicaearchia, about three days journey south of Rome. Apollonius was already within the temple when they entered it, so he had doubtlessly materialized there earlier, possibly right after he had vanished at Rome. At first Damis and Demetrius thought he was a ghost, until Apollonius held out his hand to the latter, saying:

> 'Take hold of me, and if I evade you, then I am indeed a ghost come to you from the realm of Persephone ... but if I resist your touch, then you shall persuade Damis also that I am both alive and that I have not abandoned my body.'
> 'How then,' said Demetrius, 'have you accomplished so long a journey in so small a fraction of the day?' And he proceeded to detail to them in his own words, and above all at the end of them the citation: 'For thou shalt not kill me,' and he told them exactly how he had vanished from the seat of judgment.

Apollonius eventually settled in Ephesus, where he may have died, although one version of his passing has him entering the temple of Athene at Lindus, a town on the island of Rhodes, and supernaturally disappearing there.

It is also recorded by Philostratus, that on 18 September AD 96, when Apollonius was one hundred years old, he was talking to a crowd of citizens at Ephesus when he psychically divined the murder in Rome of the hated Domitian by suddenly crying out, ' "Smite the tyrant, smite him!" then remaining silent for a moment, before adding, "Take heart, gentlemen, for the tyrant has been slain this day ... at the moment I uttered my words, and then lapsed into silence." ' And it was later proved that Domitian had been stabbed to death in his palace bedroom, at that time, by four assassins. In fact Apollonius's awareness of the event is still one of the most remarkable examples of clairvoyance on record.

These ancient supernatural disappearances provide us with the full range of possible variations of the phenomenon. With Cleomedes, for example, we have a living man who vanishes and who does not return, while with Caius Flaminius, it is his corpse that disappears for ever. Usually, however, the person who vanishes reappears, sometimes many miles away. This instantaneous shift from one place to another is termed translocation or teleportation, and, although not always occurring, tends to be as much a part of the phenomenon as the disappearance itself. The movement may be a matter of a few yards, as in the case of Drusus Caius, or many miles. Romulus was probably teleported about two miles; Aristeas about six miles; Apollonius thirty-five miles in the first instance, and about ninety miles in the second; while Pythagorus was translocated approximately 200 miles, which is the straight line distance between Metapontum and Taurominium – and back again!

The vanishing of Romulus is attended by a darkness and/or by a cloud, and he reappears soon afterwards in a more glorious (but apparently spiritual) form to impart a last message; Aristeas dies and then disappears, but reappears alive soon afterwards at a distant place, unlike Caius Flaminius, whose corpse also vanishes but who does not reappear; Cleomedes, the mad boxer, vanishes while being threatened with death. He too is never seen again. Drusus Caius, when a baby, is spontaneously transported to another, and higher, part of his house.

Only Pythagoras and Apollonius had any control over their disappearances, which they used as a way of getting instantly to where they wanted to be, although the supernatural visit of Apollonius to Ephesus was seemingly brought about more by his concern for those suffering from the plague than by direct will-power.

None of these cases, however, is unique, for even the most curious of them, the disappearance of Aristeas as a corpse and his reappearance as a living man, has its parallel in the resurrection of Jesus Christ.

The intense stress caused by fear of death may have been the main factor in the supernatural disappearance of Cleomedes, and it may well have contributed to the post-mortem vanishing of Caius Flaminius. Romulus's disappearance during an eclipse, which was partnered by a thunderstorm, suggests that one or both events may have brought it about.

However, because we have many more strange disappearances and reappearances to examine, it seems best to wait before speculating further upon the causes of them. Yet the reader might like to ponder why, when many people are subject to the same conditions, only one of them, if any, supernaturally disappears?

2　Devilish Movements

The Maid was removed strangely, in the Twinkling of an Eye, out of Bed, sometimes into the Bottom of a Chest with Linnen, and the Linnen not at all disordered; sometimes betwixt the two Beds she lay on; sometimes under a Parcell of Wooll; sometimes betwixt his bed and the Mat of it in another room; and, once, she was laid on a small Deal Board which lay on top of an House between two Solar Beams, where he was forc'd to rear up ladders to have her fetch'd down.

Testimony from the trial for witchcraft of Florence Newton,
1661

It is ironic that in later years, when paganism was swept away by Christianity, the phenomenon of the supernatural disappearance, and the frequent accompanying translocation to a distant spot of the person concerned, was regarded as the Devil's work, or was blamed on mischievous beings like the fairies.

While these beliefs were of no importance to the person who vanished and was never seen again, they often had unfortunate consequences for the teleportees, as a charge of Devil-worship, witchcraft or even black magic was invariably lodged against them, which was very difficult for them, no matter how innocent, to refute.

A quite remarkable and distressing case of apparent long-distance teleportation is mentioned by the antiquary and folklorist John Aubrey (1626–1697) in his *Miscellanies*. Published in 1696, the year before Aubrey died, *Miscellanies* is one of the first books devoted to psychic research, and in the chapter entitled 'Transportation by an Invisible Power' its author briefly and intriguingly records that 'A gentleman of my acquaintance, Mr M., was in Portugal, anno, 1655, when one was burnt by the inquisition for being brought hither from Goa, in East-India, in the air, in an incredible short time.'

The distance between Goa and Lisbon is about 5,000 miles, and we can be reasonably sure that the unnamed man was not transported through the air by lateral levitation, which would almost certainly have brought about his death, but was instantly moved between those two places by teleportation. His burning at the stake means that he was found guilty of having made a pact with the Devil to accomplish such an incredible feat, and unfortunately the doubtlessly nonplussed traveller had no defence except to protest his innocence. Yet that was of course precluded by his aerial journey.

However, if such a long-distance movement by teleportation sounds totally impossible, there is a well-authenticated case which proves that such an unlikely thing can happen. This time it ended happily for the bemused victim. The astounding event took place in the early evening of 24 October 1593, when a soldier clad in an unfamiliar uniform tried to join those on guard outside the Governor's Palace in the Plaza Mayor, Mexico City. His manner was confused and uncertain, and he stared about him like a lost child. He was immediately asked by the officer in charge to give an account of himself. After some hesitation, he answered in a shaking voice:

> My name is Gil Perez. As to standing here, I am doing as nearly as possible what I was ordered to do. I was ordered this morning to mount guard at the doors of the Governor's Palace in Manila. I know very well that this is not the Governor's Palace, and evidently I am not in Manila. Why or how that may be, I know not. But here I am, and this is a palace of some kind, so I am doing my duty as nearly as possible.

He went on to add that, 'Last night the Governor of the Filipinas, His Excellency Don Gomez Perez Dasmarinas, had his head cracked with an axe in the Moluccas and is dead of it.'

Gil Perez was stunned when he was told that he was now in Mexico City, half a world away from the Philippines, and he would not at first believe it. Yet when it was made plain to him that this was true, he could only repeat his story about being detailed to mount guard outside the Governor's Palace in Manila. He had absolutely no idea as to how or why he now found himself in Mexico City, nor any memory of being conveyed there. It was a complete and utter mystery to him.

Inquiries were immediately made by the viceroy and other authorities in Mexico City, who soon established that Perez was wearing a uniform of the Governor of Manila's guard. Yet it was clearly impossible, they thought, for him to have come from Manila in such a short time, unless he had received help from the Devil. The suspicion that Perez might have enjoyed diabolical assistance led to him being handed over to the Holy Office, whose priests re-examined him, but without being able to persuade him to admit to any occult involvement. In fact Gil Perez stuck resolutely to his story: he had been brought to Mexico City from Manila entirely against his will, and certainly without signing a pact with the Devil. All he knew was that he had been about to take up his guard duties in the early morning of 25 October 1593 outside the Governor's Palace in Manila, when he suddenly found himself in Mexico City on the evening of 24 October, which being some fourteen hours behind Manila not only accounted for the difference in date but meant that his transportation there was instantaneous. The Holy Office, impressed by his testimony and recognizing that something diabolical yet seemingly involuntary had taken place, had Perez placed in jail for safe keeping while further inquiries were made.

Verification of the man's remarkable story came about two months later, when a ship arrived from the Philippines bringing news that the Governor of Manila had been murdered with an axe on 23 October, the day before Gil Perez's arrival, and a passenger who knew that Perez was a member of the Palace Guard and who swore to having seen him in Manila on the day before he turned up in Mexico City. This substantiated all that Perez had said, and the Holy Office in turn decided that while the Devil was probably the cause of Perez's instantaneous journey half-way around the world, Perez himself was not to blame for this and was therefore an unwitting victim of a devilish prank. Gil Perez was therefore freed from jail and pardoned, and was later returned to the Philippines to resume his life as a palace guard.

Gil Perez was fortunate indeed to have escaped being burned at the stake, as punishment by torture and by *auto-da-fé*, or alternatively by hanging, drawing and quartering, were the general lot of those Christians found guilty of occult or magical practices. In fact, unlike the ancient Greeks, who believed that supernatural phenomena were caused by the gods, Christians regarded them as demonic in origin. Hence it was generally accepted that only those who practised witchcraft or who worshipped the Devil could gain supernatural powers or experience such marvels as levitation and translocation.

Yet the earliest Christians, like the Jews before them, were less fixated by the Evil One. The change of view, of regarding supernatural acts as devilish rather than divine, started during the third and fourth centuries AD, when Christianity became the dominant religion of the Mediterranean world. For once paganism ceased to be Christianity's rival and enemy, a loss that robbed Christians of a stone to hone and shine themselves against, they quickly substituted the Devil for the old gods, while shifting 'evil' from the external to the internal, which enabled them to identify all those human needs and temptations, like lust, greed, ambition and vanity, to which they were all subject, with the Arch-Tempter and Deceiver, who constantly sought to lure all humanity into his clutches with them, and thus into hell.

We find this struggle with the Devil taking what was to become its characteristic form among those Christians who cut themselves off from the rest of society, by becoming monks, nuns, and hermits. These pious folk went to live in deserts and other inhospitable places, where they hoped, by distancing themselves from the temptations of town and city life, to get closer to God. Yet for many, denied as they were the ordinary pleasures of existence, their fight to obtain perfection became more difficult, not less. This could only be explained by saying that the Devil was actively wrestling with them for the possession of their souls, 'targeting' them if you like, his prime objective being to trip them up and make them his own. The monks and nuns often made things worse for themselves by developing their own rivalries and jealousies – competitive fasting, for instance, was common among them – which sometimes meant that those who developed supernatural powers, as many did, found themselves being accused of commerce with the Devil, instead of being looked upon as specially favoured by God.

This explains why the fourth-century ascetic Abba Pachomius, who founded a monastery at Tabenna in the Egyptian desert, scorned a monk who claimed to have walked, like Jesus, on water:

He is able to pass over the river [he thundered] as one who travelleth over dry land through the neglect of God, and the Calumniator helpeth him ... I devote all my strivings, and all my anxious care, not that I may pass over the river by walking on the waters thereof, but in trying to flee from the judgement of God, and to escape, by the might of the Lord, from such Satanic wiles as these.

Yet sometimes the desire to resist the Devil and all his works resulted in some amazing occurrences. One of the most interesting from our point of view happened in the desert of Scete, which lies to the west of the Nile delta, a region wherein numerous monks and hermits settled. Of these, some belonged to communities which had their own rules and way of life, while others preferred to lead solitary lives. Where the latter were concerned, it was common for an old monk or nun to take a younger companion as his or her student and helpmate. Such lives were rigorous and secluded, yet highly spiritual, and it is not surprising to find that many who pursued them developed psychic powers beyond the ordinary, to the extent of their being able to perform, at least on occasions, supernatural acts or miracles.

A monk named Palladius visited many of these remote communities and solitary individuals at the end of the fourth century of our era, and he wrote about his travels and the people he met in a work entitled *Paradise* or the *Lausiac History*, which was composed in AD 420 at the urging of one Lausus, a high-ranking official in Constantinople, who accounts for its alternative title.

Of particular interest to us, among the many remarkable stories he tells, is the experience that befell a young disciple, noted for his obedience, who lived with an aged monk in the Scete desert. The pair worked together at making palm-leaf mats and baskets, which the young man would on occasion take to the nearest village to sell or barter for the food and other provisions that they needed. But unfortunately the young man was horrified to discover that he began having lascivious thoughts when visiting the village, particularly with regard to an attractive young virgin who frequently bought items from him and who flirted with him. Lust, of course, was the principal temptation that young desert-dwellers had to guard against, yet the disciple did not know whether to refuse to go to the village, which would mean committing the sin of disobedience, or expose himself to the delights of the flesh and risk falling into the sin of fornication.

The young man therefore took the sensible course of discussing his problem with a brother monk living in the village, who strengthened his resolve by telling him that the Devil was more interested in making him disobedient than he was in tempting him into fornication, and by advising: 'Go therefore, O my son, and obey thy father unhesitatingly, and when the war cometh upon thee say thus: "O God of my father, help me!"'

When the young disciple next visited the village Palladius records that:

> SATAN stirred up that woman to go forth to greet him as it were by chance, and having seen that brother and being inflamed through the operation of SATAN with the fire of love for him, she drew nigh unto him by means of some crafty device, and took him and brought him into her house, with the excuse that she was going to buy something from him; and after they had gone in, and she had shut the door upon them, she began to throw herself upon him. Then that brother, with faith wherein there was no doubt, cried out in a loud voice and said, 'O God of my father, help me!' And immediately, by the agency of God, he found himself on the road to SCETE, and by the Divine help the Calumniator was put to shame, and the war of fornication ceased from that brother.

We are unfortunately given no account of the psychological after-effects that such a rapid and unexpected translocation had on the young man, other than it put him off sex for life, although his disappearance from the woman's house and his reappearance on the road to Scete did not seemingly cause him to lose consciousness. Nor are we told how his vanishing in front of her eyes affected the young woman. The shock of it might have rendered her frigid!

Like the young man from Scete, several Catholic saints have reputedly been teleported from one place to another, although all were fortunate in avoiding the charge of Devil worship. They include St Anthony of Padua (1195–1231), who thus travelled, it is said, from Padua, where he was preaching the gospel, to Lisbon, a distance of about 1,250 miles, to defend his father, who had been unjustly accused of murder; St Peter of Alcantara (1499–1562), the Spanish mystic, who was translocated about 300 miles from Madrid to the province of Estremadura in Portugal; and St Columba of Rieti, who vanished from his mother's house in Rieti and materialized twenty miles away in a nunnery at Spoleto. St John of the Cross (1542–1591), a Spanish Carmelite, is said to have once supernaturally disappeared from his bed and to have reappeared in it sometime later, although it is not known if he stopped anywhere in between.

There is some reason to believe that the great English churchman St Dunstan (c. 909–988), who was born near Glastonbury, may have undergone a spontaneous short-distance teleportation as a boy. Apparently while Dunstan was being educated by the monks at Glastonbury, he became very ill for several weeks with 'brain fever' and it was feared that he might not recover. In his delirium his mother stayed with him, yet one night, when he had thankfully quietened down, she fell asleep with fatigue. But the delirium came upon Dunstan again, and he jumped out of bed and ran in a frenzy to the nearby church. Finding the door locked, he climbed up on to the roof by means of a ladder that had been left against the wall. What happened then is a mystery. All that is known is that when a search was made for him early the next morning, Dunstan was found lying semi-conscious within the locked church, his brain fever gone. In fact it was only after his miraculous cure that Dunstan decided to dedicate his life to God.

But while the average person, and certainly priests, abjured the occult in former times, magicians by contrast often invoked spirits or demons in their rituals and it was widely believed that flight and/or instantaneous translocation to a distant place could be achieved with their help. But because each spirit had a particular area of expertise, the magician had to make sure he called upon the right one to ensure his success. According to the *True Grimoire*, which has been called 'A book by the Devil', the demon responsible for carrying 'anyone or anything anywhere in the world' is Aglasis, who can be summoned by means of a rather long and involved magic ceremony. Another grimoire, the so-called *Book of Power*, written by the Master Aptolcater, who was evidently of Middle Eastern origin, says the spirit responsible for instant travel is the genie Ampharool. When summoned, Ampharool will give the magician a Ring of Travel, which when placed upon a finger will immediately remove him to the place where he wants to be.

Other magical methods, instead of calling upon demons, relied upon concoctions of odd and sometimes difficult to obtain ingredients mixed together at the right astrological moment to produce the desired effect. The Master Aptolcater gives one fairly straightforward recipe for instantaneous travel – which he rather pretentiously calls 'a great secret' – that requires the magician to boil snow with oil, which is then placed in a sheep's bladder, left for one and a half months, then absorbed into charcoal, which is afterwards powdered on an alabaster table and the powder placed for safe keeping in a horn. When the magician wishes to fly somewhere, he has to put a pinch of the powder between the pages of a book.

> You will then take the book and sit with it in your hand, and think of the place to which you are to fly. And this takes longer at first. And when you are ready to fly, and will feel tired, and then you say, 'SISPI, SISPI,' and you will instantly be at your destination.

Apparently for the return flight, the words 'ITTSS, ITTSS' are to be used.

Rather intriguingly, Master Aptolcater comments that in 'former times' a certain king was able to rule two countries at the same time by means of the above spell, without his subjects in either knowing that he was monarch of the other! But as the magician neither names the king nor the countries, it is impossible to verify what he says.

Flying on a broomstick to their sabbats is something that witches once did, according to one of the popular misconceptions about these much maligned people; other slanders include their hook-nosed and ugly appearance, their possession of a pet or familiar in the form of a black cat, a toad or a snake, and their worship of the Devil. Witches were also supposed to be recognizable by virtue of a distinguishing bodily contusion, such as a large or oddly shaped mole or birthmark, or by a physical abnormality like a sixth finger or toe.

The above mentioned physical traits made life very hazardous for many during the period of the European witch craze (1550–1750), when the belief in, and the fear of, witches was at its height. Aged females who possessed a cat and a broom and who talked to themselves were in particular danger, as such a combination of characteristics marked them out as witches and as Devil-worshippers.

> As I was walking with my friend Sir Roger by the side of one of his woods, an old woman applied herself to me for my charity [wrote Joseph Addison in 1711, in an attempt to draw attention to the plight of the aged poor]. The knight told me, that this very old woman had the reputation of a witch all over the country, that her lips were observed to be always in motion, and that there was not a switch about her house which her neighbours did not believe had carried her several hundreds of miles ... I was secretly concerned to see human nature in so much wretchedness and disgrace, but at the same time could not forbear smiling to hear Sir Roger, who is a little puzzled about the old woman, advising her as a justice of the peace to avoid all communication with the devil, and never to hurt any of her neighbours' cattle.

Yet despite the popular association of witchcraft with Devil-worship and with flying, it can unequivocally be said that both are false. Witches worship a female deity, known as the Great Goddess, and they do not even admit to the existence of the Devil, who is essentially a Christian bugaboo, let alone worship him. Neither do they, nor can they, fly from place to place, for as the modern witch Gerald Gardner asserted: 'No witch ever flew through the air on a broomstick or on anything else, at least not until aeroplanes came in.'

But while witches did not and could not fly to their meetings at the time of the full moon, people who spontaneously levitated, or who were teleported to a near or distant place, would inevitably be accused of witchcraft and/or Devil-worship if their incredible, though unwanted, motion was observed. The quote from the trial of Florence Newton at Cork Assizes in 1661, given at the beginning of this chapter, reveals how her amazing and marvellous translocations both within and around her home were used as evidence against her.

Teleportation and other mysterious disappearances were also

often blamed on the fairies or little people, that strange race of diminutive supernatural beings who traditionally inhabit woods, hills and other remote country areas, and who are said to possess magical or occult powers.

The two main types of fairy are the elves and the dwarves or trolls. The elves are generally considered to be human-like in appearance, yet handsomer or prettier and more finely made, and stand about elbow height. They are good-humoured and kind, wise and clever, and they like nothing better than dancing and feasting all night, especially on nights lit by the light of the moon. Indeed, they are only active at night, for sunlight is harmful to them. They are said to know the future and the whereabouts of treasure.

Dwarves, by contrast, while small, are physically repellent, either through ugliness or deformity. They characteristically have large heads, long grey beards, and a pale complexion. Dwarves are creatures of the earth, spending much of their time underground in caves, caverns and mines, and indeed they are regarded as the owners of the earth's mineral wealth, which includes buried treasure. They have great intelligence and, like the elves, they know the future. Yet they do not possess the natural benevolence of elves, and because they can be easily upset, they are more feared.

While fairies normally avoid people, they are reputed to have a fondness for human infants, whom they will snatch away if the opportunity arises. Sometimes they leave a substitute 'fairy-child' behind, although the purpose of this exchange is not known. But the old fear of parents of having their baby stolen by fairies evidently derives from the suddenness and secrecy of the thefts, which suggests that in certain instances at least the disappearance of the missing child may have been supernatural, as happened with the infant Drusus Caius.

Yet ramblers in country areas, particularly when abroad at night, may sometimes be lured to a spot by the sound of music and revelry, to find that they have stumbled upon a fairy gathering. Such events often take place in fairy rings or, alternatively, in the interior of hills. Quite often the music, like the sound of the sirens singing, is so delightful that it proves irresistible to the listener, who is thereby drawn into the fairies' midst. There he (or she) will be greeted warmly and be encouraged to take part in the celebrations. The person will then join in the dancing with abandon, and will thoroughly enjoy himself. Yet danger lies ahead, for once someone has stumbled upon fairies feasting and dancing, they will try to prevent him returning home. This is accomplished by offering him something to eat or drink. If he tastes either, he is lost and can never return. But if he resolutely refuses nourishment, he cannot be held against his will.

In the Manx fairy story *Robin the Fiddler*, recorded by the aptly named Dora Broome, the hero Robin is lured into a fairy hill within which the fairies are making merry. He plays his fiddle for them and they flatter him on his musical skill, and press him to eat the cakes and fruits, and to drink the wine, that they have in plenty. He sensibly refuses. Then:

> As he was standing in a corner, he noticed that some of the little creatures had the look of men he'd known years ago, men who were said to have gone to foreign countries, or to have been lost at sea. One of them came close to him, and pulled his sleeve.
>
> 'Don't touch anythin' Robin boy,' he whispered, 'or thou will have to stay for ever, like us.'
>
> 'Who art thou?' said Robin.
>
> 'Don't thou know me, boy?' said the little creature. 'Don't thou remember Jim Kerruish? I was big once, like thee, an' I'd a wife an' childher an' a home, but I'll never see them again, I'm sayin'.'

One of the stranger things about life in the fairy kingdom is that time there is markedly different from that outside it. A man or woman can spend what seems to be a short time there dancing, but emerges, if he or she does, to discover that a far longer period has gone by outside.

In the early nineteenth century a Welshman named Rhys was taken into a fairy circle one evening, while his travelling companion Llewellyn went on home. When Llewellyn discovered the next morning that Rhys had not returned, he went in search of him, aided by a local farmer, who knew of the fairies and their ways, and the teller of the story, and eventually managed to find Rhys and to pull him, protesting vigorously at the interruption, from the circle. It was soon discovered that Rhys thought he had only been dancing for five minutes, rather than the several hours of our time.

Scotland's most famous prophet, Thomas of Ercildoun (or Erceldoune), otherwise known as Thomas the Rhymer or True Thomas, who lived in the thirteenth century, was said to have been given his powers of foresight by the fairy queen, whom he met under a tree on the Eildon Hills and who took him with her to Elfland, 'where he abode, as he deemed, for three days, but in reality for three years', although the folk song entitled 'Thomas Rymer [sic]' portrays him as being away for seven years:

He has gotten a coat of the even cloth,
And a pair of shoes of velvet green,
And till seven years were past and gone
True Thomas on earth was never seen.

When the queen released Thomas back into our world, having given him 'a prophetic tongue that cannot lie', he knew that he would one day receive a sign that he must return to her. This came some years later, when it was reported to him that a stag and a hind had left the forest and were walking, slowly and fearlessly, up and down the street of Ercildoun. Thomas immediately rose and went to them, and followed them into the forest. From that moment he was never seen again, having, as it seems, supernaturally disappeared.

But fairies, so it is rumoured, can also transport people rapidly over long distances. This is a power particularly utilized by the fairy known as a phynnodderee, which is said to be somewhat Pan-like in appearance, having a hairy, half-human and half-bestial body, and pointed ears. He also plays a reed pipe with which he attracts animals. The phynodderee lifts those it wishes to carry away up by their hair and whisks them through the air like a blown leaf.

In the simpler, more rural societies of the past, which had a strong belief in fairies and their magic powers, it doubtless became second nature, and perhaps even convenient, to blame these mischievous beings for spiriting away people who had run off or been abducted, or who had been murdered. Yet at the same time the tales about fairies are legion and found throughout the world, which in itself suggests that there is more to them than Scotch mist. I do not wish to argue the case one way or the other, but it does seem to me that many of the stories of disappearances involving fairies may be based on actual vanishings, which have found a ready-made, understandable explanation in the activities of the little people. It is, after all, psychologically easier to cope with a disappearance that has a known causal agent, like the fairies, than one which seems totally inexplicable.

John Aubrey tells a fascinating story of a man's translocation to a distant place, which a Scottish friend informed him about in a letter written on 25 March 1695. The friend, known only by his initials J.G., says he heard the story 'a long time ago' and that it happened to one of Lord Duffus's ancestors. It is of interest to us because it demonstrates how the fairies were thought responsible for his being carried away:

> It is reported, that upon a time, when he was walking abroad in the fields near to his own house [in Murrayshire], he was suddenly carried away, and found the next day at Paris in the French King's cellar, with a silver cup in his hand; that being brought into the King's presence and questioned by him, who he was? and how he came hither? he told his name, his country, and the place of his residence, and that on such a day of the month [which proved to be the day immediately preceding] being in the fields, he heard a noise of a whirl-wind, and of voices crying *Horse and Hattock*, [this is the word which the fairies are said to use when they remove from any place] whereupon he cried [Horse and Hattock] also, and was immediately caught up, and transported through the air, by the fairies of that place, where after he had drank heartily he fell asleep, and before he awoke, the rest of the company were gone, and had left him in posture wherein he was found.

Lastly, the power of melody in the form of birdsong to alter the passage of time, like the fairy music already mentioned, is recorded in the curious legend of a twelfth-century monk who mysteriously vanished from his own era while listening to a nightingale. The monk, who lived at Basingwerk Abbey, in Greenfield, Clwyd, went for a walk in a nearby wood, where he heard a nightingale singing. He was so entranced by the delightful sound that he stayed to listen to it for what seemed like several hours. Yet when he finally tore himself away and returned to the abbey, he found to his horror that it was in a state of ruin and that the people he met were all strangers, who were dressed in clothes the like of which he had never seen before. He went up to a small group of them to ask who they were and what had happened, and was puzzled to find that they did not take kindly to his questions. They were villagers, they retorted, and the abbey, to their recollection, had always been like that. Then one of them commented that his sudden coming among them put him in mind of a monk from the abbey who had unaccountably disappeared several centuries before. The monk, having turned pale at this and looking thin and wasted, was then offered some food by the villagers. He reached out to take it, but as the food touched his fingers he was instantly turned to dust!

3   Mysterious Appearances

By my living soul, Lord King, and by your living soul, too, I did not have relations with any man to make me bear this child. I know only this: that, when I was in our private apartments with my sister nuns, some one used to come to me in the form of a most handsome young man. He would often hold me tightly in his arms and kiss me. When he had been some little time with me he would disappear, so that I could no longer see him. Many times, too, when I was sitting alone, he would talk with me, without becoming visible; and when he came to see me in this way he would often make love with me, as a man would do, and in that way he made me pregnant.

From *The History of the Kings of Britain* by Geoffrey of
Monmouth

In the first chapter I examined a number of early supernatural disappearaces, two of which are distinguished by the fact that the person concerned is never seen again, while in the others he reappears as if by magic in another place, which may be many miles away from the site of his vanishing.

However, there is one very interesting ancient case that is rather different from those discussed, in that it has a supernatural disappearance and an appearance happening together. It is also important because the person who disappeared was not only dead, like Caius Flaminius, but a woman, thereby demonstrating that men are not the only people who can vanish into thin air!

The woman was an ancient Greek queen named Alcmene, who was the wife of King Amphitryon of Mycenae and mother to the famous strong-man Heracles. Following her husband's and then her son's unfortunate deaths, Alcmene settled in the city of

Thebes, where she died from natural causes at an advanced age, in about 1200 BC.

The death of such a celebrated woman and queen called for a lavish public funeral, at which her grandchildren, known as the Heraclids, carried her coffin from the palace where her body had lain on public view, through the city streets to the graveyard, watched by the mourning citizens of Thebes.

All went well until the Heraclids, on nearing the graveyard, suddenly felt the coffin increase in weight, to such an extent that, becoming fatigued, they were obliged to lay it down. Curiosity and puzzlement then prompted them to open it, and what they saw inside had them leaping back in stunned alarm, for Alcmene's body had mysteriously vanished and its place had been taken by a large rock!

It was not long before a divine explanation was formulated to explain the amazing happening. Father Zeus, it was said, had ordered the god Hermes to substitute a rock for Alcmene's corpse as the funeral procession wound its way through the streets of Thebes, in order that Zeus might carry her away to the Islands of the Blessed. The materialized rock, being of supposedly divine origin, was erected in a sacred grove outside Thebes, at which Alcmene was worshipped as a goddess.

We cannot of course know where the rock came from. It may have supernaturally vanished from some nearby (or even distant) rocky slope at the same moment Alcmene's body disappeared, to then rematerialize within her empty coffin. Or it may have disappeared from some other dimension of being and somehow crossed the gulf which separates that world from our own.

In fact there are a number of cases where a supernatural appearance is not, or at least as far as we know, preceded by the appearant's supernatural disappearance in our world. And because the manifesting person or object may bring some spiritual benefit to those who witness his or its arrival, as happened with the rock that took Alcmene's place, such arrivals may indeed be 'messengers' from another realm.

This certainly happened in the last ancient case I shall consider, which took place among the Etruscans, a people who occupied the fertile plain now known as Tuscany, lying between the rivers Tiber and Arno in Italy.

Shortly after the Etruscans had arrived in Italy from their

homeland in Lydia, a migration which probably took place some-time during the seventh century BC, a farmer named Tarchon was ploughing in his fields outside the town of Tarquinia. Suddenly, either as a result of him ploughing too deeply or by upturning a particular clod of earth, Tarchon was stunned to see a small humanoid being emerge from the furrow (or from the clod), which had the face and stature of a child but the grey hair and bearing of an old man. The frightened farmer shouted to his neighbours, who quickly ran over to see what had happened, and at their arrival the dwarf spoke, saying that his name was Tages and that he was the grandson of the great god Tinia (the Etruscan Jupiter), who had sent him there expressly to teach them how to live. He then imparted to the Etruscans a body of knowledge known as the Tagetic Doctrine, hurriedly inscribed by his listeners on to wax tablets, which outlined the laws of property, the nature of the gods and the structure of the universe, and a technique, called *haruspicy* or liver-reading, for divining the future. That done, the dwarf stepped back into the furrow and vanished.

This of course sounds a totally improbable story and one at which you might be tempted to laugh. But the Etruscans, who were a remarkably pious people, believed in it as implicitly as devout Christians believe in the life and teachings of Jesus Christ. In fact Tages, for them, was a divine messenger like Jesus, and bore a similar patrilineal relationship to Tinia, being his grandson, as Jesus did to God his father. This should perhaps persuade us that Tages did manifest among the Etruscans in the manner described, and that his coming, brief though it was, was the pivotal event of Etruscan history, about which everything in their society revolved.

A startling supernatural appearance once happened before Pachomius, the monk whom we met in the last chapter, and a brother monk named Theodore, while they were walking one night through the monastery at Tabenna. Quite suddenly, to their surprise and alarm, a woman manifested in front of them. She was indescribably beautiful to look at, and as she came 'nearer and nearer [she] took on a solid form'. She then spoke to the two monks and told them that she was the daughter of the Devil, although she rather contrarily added that she had 'received power from God, who sustaineth the universe, to tempt whomsoever I please; and I have abundance of time in which to do this, for this I have asked from God'.

But having talked more about her purpose, which was simply to inflame holy men like Pachomius and Theodore with lust, the woman let on that if she and her fellow devils were resisted 'we dissolve away even as smoke is dissipated in the air'. Upon which Pachomius instructed her to go and never to darken his monastery door again, whereupon she vanished in the manner she had described.

Pachomius described the incident as a 'vision', yet if the woman became solid she was more than that, and we can perhaps regard her as a real person. But how she managed to manifest in the way she did and where she came from is impossible to say. She may have been teleported into Pachomius's and Theodore's presence from somewhere in this world, or she may have come from another dimension of being altogether. However, because she did not try to touch and kiss the monks, or to otherwise excite them, her words and her supposed function as a temptress may have been projected on to her by the two sexually frustrated men, who were disturbed by her femininity and her loveliness.

One of the most remarkable of all supernatural appearances, that of two green-coloured children, happened many centuries later in England during either the reign of King Stephen (1135–1154) or that of his successor, Henry II (1154–1189).

Although the children's arrival did not spiritually uplift or benefit those who met them, it did give them (and us) an opportunity to learn what life is like in the dimension from which they came. The incident was first recorded by William of Newburgh (1136–1201) in his *Historia Rerum Angliarum*, about which the *Dictionary of National Biography* comments:

In substance and in form William's book is the finest historical work left to us by an Englishman of the twelfth century ... he tells, indeed, some marvellous tales of the supernatural; but on some of these he expressly suspends his judgment; and all of them he relates, not as mere marvels, but as matters for which there has been put before him such an overwhelming weight or volume of testimony that he feels bound, by his undertaking to put on record all that he can of 'the memorable things of our time' not to exclude them from his pages.

According to William of Newburgh, one harvest peasants

reaping corn in fields near to the village of Woolpit in Suffolk, were startled to see two children with green skin walking towards them. The children, a boy and a girl, came from the direction of some old trenches known as 'Wlfpittes', into which captured wolves had once been thrown and from which the village derives its name. The peasants, overcoming their fear, quickly took hold of the pair, who were crying and confused, and whose strange dress-like clothing they found to be made from a material that was unfamiliar to them.

The children were brought to the village, offered some food, which they refused, and eventually given a home by Sir Richard de Calne, who resided at nearby Wikes. In fact the green children would not eat anything for several days, until finally their hunger prompted them to try some beans, which they discovered they greatly liked and on which they subsisted for many months. Yet despite this care, the strangeness of their surroundings and the evident shock that it had had on them, soon resulted in the boy's death. The girl, however, survived and gradually adjusted to her new environment. As time went by her green colour faded, and she acquired instead a pink complexion.

Neither of the children when found could speak English, but the girl eventually learned enough to explain where she and her brother, for such he was, came from. Their homeland, she said, was a country named St Martin, which lay beside a broad river that the inhabitants did not know how to cross. It was a twilight land, because unlike the county of Suffolk, it did not have a sun in the sky. Yet some illumination came to St Martin from across the river, where there was a land of light. The people, who all had a green colour, were Christians, and in other respects their lives were similar to those led by the inhabitants of Wikes and Woolpit. On the day of their disappearance from St Martin, the girl said that she and her brother had been taking care of their father's sheep, when suddenly they heard a loud noise, whereupon they found themselves close by the wolf pits near Woolpit.

Gervase of Tilbury, who also writes of these strange children, represents the girl as saying:

We are folk of St Martin's Land; for he is the chief saint among us. We know not where the land is, and remember only that one day we were feeding our father's flock in the field when we heard a great noise like bells, as when, at St Edmunds, they all peal together. And on a sudden we were both caught up in the spirit and found ourselves in your harvest-field. Among us no sun riseth, nor is there open sunshine, but such a twilight as here goes before the rising and setting of the sun. Yet there is a land of light to be seen not far from us, but cut off from us by a stream of great width.

Another contemporary writer, Abbot Ralph of Coggeshall, gives a different account of the green children's arrival at Woolpit. He says that the girl

asked in what manner she had come from the land, aforesaid, with the boy, she replied that they were following sheep, and arrived at a certain cavern. On entering it they heard a certain delectable sound of bells and, in trying to reach the sweet sound, they wandered for a very long time through the cavern until they came to its end. Thence, emerging, the excessive brightness of our sun and the unwonted, warm temperature of our air astonished and terrified them. And for a long time they lay upon the edge of the cave. When overcome with disquietude, they wished to flee, but they could not in the least find the entrance to the cavern, until they were seized by the people of the countryside.

The girl was eventually employed as a servant in de Calne's household, where she lived for some time. Abbot Ralph adds the interesting footnote that, growing into adulthood, 'she showed herself very wanton and lascivious', and in due course she married a man of King's Lynn in Norfolk. It is believed that she resided at King's Lynn with her husband for many years, although it is not know if she had any children by him, or indeed what happened to her thereafter.

It is difficult to know quite what to make of this remarkable story. Yet if it is essentially true, and William of Newburgh is said to have spoken to several people who had known the green children, then it is one of the greatest mysteries of all time. For the children could not have come from some then unknown country, as there is nowhere that has green inhabitants or a continual twilight such as they described, yet none the less St Martin evidently had many things in common with our world, such as the general physical type of its people, who are in essence green-coloured Europeans, their way of life, their sheep, their churches and their Christianity. Ralph of Coggeshall's version of the children's arrival via an underground cavern suggests that St Martin lies beneath Suffolk, although such a subterranean world, if it existed, would really be pitch black and it would certainly have no sky overhead similar to, but darker than, our own.

It may perhaps be, therefore, that St Martin really exists in another dimension of being and time altogether, one which mimics our own in many ways, yet differs from it in several important respects. Physicists have postulated that there are such parallel universes, which exist alongside, as it were, our own, but which are completely separate from it. If so, the green children were unfortunate enough to have been 'caught up in the spirit' in their world, from which they supernaturally disappeared, sent thereby across the divide which exists between their dimension and ours, and then rematerialized in a harvest-field outside Woolpit. And if that could happen to them, then there may well be a movement of people in the opposite direction, which suggests that some of those who supernaturally vanish from our world may be translocated to another dimension, one from which they can never return.

It is said that these green children are not the only ones to have come to our world, as two others, one male and one female, supposedly emerged from a cave outside the town of Banjos, Spain, in August 1887. They too were reported to have been dressed in clothes made from an unknown material, and, like the Woolpit children, they were very frightened and upset by their strange surroundings. They spoke a language that was totally unknown to their listeners, and they had no knowledge of Spanish. However, in contrast to the Woolpit children, who had European features, they had slanted eyes like those of an Oriental.

Again, these green children at first refused to touch the food which was offered to them, but were eventually driven to eat it by hunger. The boy also soon died, but the girl survived to learn some Spanish, and told her rescuers that they had lived in a land without a sun, from which they were one day swept away by a whirlwind and deposited in the cave. Yet the girl did not live much beyond puberty, for she died, so the story goes, in 1892.

This supernatural appearance, however, is almost certainly

spurious, being simply the transference of the green children of Woolpit to Banjos, although how that happened is anyone's guess. As we shall see, the movement of unusual incidents to places far from where they actually occurred often happens – by a process that is often more mysterious than the incident itself – and which makes getting at the truth a tedious and time-consuming business, for so many seemingly true stories, which have often been seriously discussed by well-known writers, prove to be nothing more than mirages.

From time to time animals, plants, and non-living objects also appear as if from nowhere. Such materializations are most commonly encountered in seance rooms, where they are supposedly brought by spirits and which in turn gives them their name – apports, from the French *apporter*, meaning 'to bring'. There are likewise numerous accounts collected from around the world by people like Charles Fort, of objects falling from the sky, which include not only stones and lumps of ice, but also showers of live frogs, snakes, eels, snails, fish and dead birds, as well as various types of vegetable matter.

The July 1987 *Society for Psychical Research Newsletter* records two separate object materializations witnessed by a correspondent. In the first, a piece of wood manifested, and in the second, a number of 2p coins. The man (whose identity is not revealed) writes of the former incident:

> I was sitting at the table in [my] office when before my eyes about two feet away a piece of wood materialized out of thin air and floated silently to the ground. I picked it up and found it to be a perfectly normal piece of wood. What I noticed particularly was that it fell at constant velocity, not accelerating as an object normally does under gravity.

On the second occasion, which also took place in the man's office, four 2p coins separately manifested, each being preceded by a loud noise resembling a pistol shot. At first the man thought the startling sounds resulted from the coins hitting the glass partition behind his desk, but on running for safety to the doorway and looking back into the room 'there was another loud crack and I was fortunate enough to actually see a coin materialize out of thin air and slowly drop to the ground. I then realized the noise I had heard was not that of coins hitting the glass but that of the coins materializing'.

These supernatural appearances, which resemble apport phenomena of the seance room, took place, the correspondent noted, when a younger male colleague was in the vicinity, who may therefore have been the psychic, although unwitting, cause of them. Certainly they and the other happenings described stopped completely when he left the firm.

However, although the arrival of apports is frequently reported in seance rooms, their 'manifestation' is often fraudulent, which is why I shall not discuss them further. Even third-rate conjuring skills are sufficient to deceive the hopeful believer. I have, for example, attended seances where the phenomena – 'spirit' voices, 'levitating' trumpets, 'apported' roses and cheap trinkets – were so obviously faked, that it seemed unbelievable to me that others in the darkened room would be taken in by them. But they were! Such indeed is the power of self-deception.

The descent of objects from the sky is, by contrast, well-documented and intriguing, yet while it is often hard to account for a shower of, say, snakes or toads, it seems that they are more likely to result from being uplifted from their natural habitat and carried to a distant site by winds, than be caused by some form of supernatural dissemination. This is not to say that supernatural object-showers never occur, but only that it is virtually impossible to distinguish those with a supernatural origin from those which the elements have somehow brought about. I shall not therefore consider such anomalous downfalls here, particularly as they have been dealt with at length by other writers.

Yet of particular interest are objects that have been lost in an ordinary way, and which then supernaturally reappear from out of nowhere, often many miles from the place where they went missing, so reuniting them with their owners.

The classic example of this phenomenon is described by the English writer Gervase of Tilbury in his *Otia Imperialia*, published in 1212. He records that a Bristol merchant had sailed to Ireland a few years earlier, leaving his wife and children at home. One morning when the ship was many miles out to sea, the man took breakfast with his crew:

After eating, he washed his knife in the salt water over the ship's side. Suddenly, the knife slipped from his hand. Now at the same hour, at Bristol, the knife fell in through the roof-window, which men call a dormer, and in his own house stuck in the table, at which his wife was then sitting. She was dumbfounded at so strange a thing, and recognizing this well-known knife laid it aside. Long after, she learned, on her husband's return, that the incident happened on the very day when she found the knife.

The author and mystic Wellesley Tudor Pole experienced a similar happening, which he mentions in his book *The Silent Road*, although the lost object did not supernaturally reappear for about three months.

In 1918, while on duty with the British Army at Haifa, in Israel, Major Pole was presented with a signet ring by the Bahai leader Abdul Baha Abbas, whose protection he had organized. The ring was inscribed in Persian with the names and titles of God, and had been specially blessed by Abdul Baha. It was a much-valued gift, and Pole wore it constantly from then on.

However, in November of that year, while sailing on the Nile with a pair of aristocratic visitors from England, whom he was entertaining for the day, Pole accidentally dropped the ring into the river. The conditions pertaining to its loss were unusual. He was steering the felucca at the time, and as the party approached Cairo, their destination, an Egyptian would-be assassin fired at Pole from a nearby island, narrowly missing him. At that moment there was a strong gust of wind, which caught the sail and whipped around the boat, causing him to reach out for a stray length of rope. It was then that the ring, being somewhat loose, slipped from his finger and fell into the deepest part of the river.

Pole was very upset by the ring's unfortunate loss, and he prayed each day thereafter for its recovery. Then, towards the end of February 1919, while he was in his office at the British Military HQ in Cairo, his prayers were suddenly and unexpectedly answered. This is what happened:

One late afternoon, at about the same time as my ring had fallen into the Nile three months before, I was sitting at my desk in shirt-sleeves, the double windows of my room being wide open. Suddenly a shot rang out, apparently fired from a balcony across the street. The bullet missed me by two feet or so and embedded itself in the wall facing the window. At that very moment my ring fell down upon the blotter on the desk in front of me with a sharp thud. It was intact in every way and is still in my possession.

Although neither the Bristol merchant's knife nor W. Tudor Pole's ring were seen to disappear by the people who dropped them, other than lose themselves beneath the surface of deep bodies of water, it is clear that both must have undergone a dematerialization in that water and then been shifted through space for a distance of many miles before suddenly materializing again, in a place that allowed them to be recovered. This happened more or less instantly in the case of the merchant's knife, whereas there was a delay of about three months where the ring was concerned. We do not know if the ring dematerialized at the time it was dropped and was then held in some form of non-physical limbo until it supernaturally manifested in Pole's office, or if it lay on the bottom of the Nile for three months. Yet because Pole makes no mention of the recovered ring having acquired any form of aquatic accretion, which it would almost certainly have done if it had remained submerged for that length of time, we may perhaps assume that the former alternative occurred. It is also interesting to note that although the knife was immediately translocated to the merchant's home in Bristol, the man himself was not physically reunited with it until his return about three months later, which is the length of time that Pole was separated from his ring.

W. Tudor Pole makes the observation, which is perhaps relevant, that his ring supernaturally appeared in his office when the conditions there closely approximated those in which it was lost, which may mean that they somehow contributed to the ring's materialization. He writes: 'The hour of the day, the weather, and the transit of the bullet were all repeated, the main difference being of course that the loss took place in the water and in the open air, and the recovery took place on land and in a room.'

On a broader canvas, the so-called Green Meadows of Enchantment fall into the category of mysteriously appearing objects. These are islands that from time to time are said to manifest in the Bristol Channel between Somerset and Pembroke, although they never appear to those who try to find them. They are said to be inhabited by fairies. The islands were once reached by some sailors in the nineteenth century, who landed and joined the fairies in their wild dances. Yet when the exhausted sailors finally took to their boat again and directed it out to sea, they turned to look back at the Green Meadows of Enchantment only to discover that they had vanished from sight. The heartbroken mariners never found them again. Thus it is hardly surprising that these transient islands are described as legendary!

However, there are many islands that have made sudden appearances but which remain very solidly in place after surfacing. Almost all of these are of volcanic origin. Some of them acquire origin myths, like the island of Thera in the Aegean Sea, which was said to have arisen from a clod of earth thrown into the water by Euphemus, one of the Argonauts, and which was later colonized by his descendants, led by one Theras, who gave it his name.

The Canadian writer and folklorist Helen Creighton came across several Nova Scotians who had had odd experiences involving islands. One told her of a sailor who, having been landed by his shipmates on L'île à Frisée, over which he took an exploratory walk, suddenly found a small but lovely garden filled with flowers standing amid an otherwise rocky and barren landscape. He entered the garden in amazement and smelled with delight the enticing fragrances; then, eager to show the garden to his fellow crewmen, he hurried back to the shore and called to them to join him. When some rowed across from the ship, he took them back the way he had come, only to discover that the garden was nowhere to be found. All trace of it had completely vanished.

On another occasion, according to Creighton, two men, whom she identifies only as Joe and Arthur, went for a ramble on tiny Duck island, lying off the east coast of Nova Scotia, when to their horror they came across a human leg bone on the beach. They were at a loss as to what to do with it, but thinking that it had probably been washed ashore, they decided while eating lunch that it would be best to bury it. Yet when they returned to the spot where they had made their grim discovery, they could not find the bone anywhere. It had simply and inexplicably vanished. 'There wasn't a dog or a crow on the island to have carried it away, nor any other human being,' observed one of them, who asked puzzledly: 'Where had it come from, and where did it go?'

The supernatural appearance of buildings happens more

frequently than might be expected, but because they seldom remain where they appear for any length of time, they are usually explained away as either phantoms or hallucinations.

Yet the buildings which have been seen, and sometimes also touched and even entered, are quite real to those who come across them, as are their often rather unusual inhabitants.

In 1933 Mr and Mrs Clifford Pye were on holiday in Cornwall. One day they travelled by bus from Wadebridge to the village of Boscastle, where they planned to stay the night. When the bus reached the top of the hill overlooking Boscastle, it stopped briefly outside a large and attractive guest-house, which so took their fancy that when they reached Boscastle and found no accommodation in the village to equal it, Mrs Pye walked back up the hill to try and book rooms there, leaving her husband behind with their luggage. Some time later she returned, hot and bothered, complaining that she could not find the guest-house. Her husband, convinced that she had no sense of distance, then irritably led her up the hill to show her where it was. Yet to his complete amazement, when they reached the site where he was certain the guest-house had been, he found that there was only an empty field. Both then realized that the pleasant guest-house and its grounds had apparently vanished into thin air! Subsequent enquiries made by them locally revealed that there was no property of that description anywhere in the neighbourhood. The guest-house had apparently materialized just for them, but disappeared before they could make use of it.

It is easy to dismiss the Pyes' experience as an hallucination brought on by their wish to find somewhere suitable to stay, one generated by need and desire. Yet this is hardly a credible explanation. Hallucinations of this type are only brought on *in extremis*, so to speak, a condition that neither of the Pyes were in. After all, they had no reason to fear that they would not find accommodation in Boscastle, and in this they were quite right. They also saw exactly the same scene, which of course they would if they were looking at the same external three-dimensional structure, but which surely would not happen if they were both generating their own visionary image. And for them to hallucinate at precisely the same time is equally unlikely. Alternatively, the guest-house might really have been a ghost house, an intangible phantom that just happened to reveal itself to the Pyes as they passed by. But if so, how did it manage to appear so solid and permanent to them? Nothing betrayed it for one moment as being ethereal. This suggests it was not a phantom but an actuality, which supernaturally appeared and then mysteriously vanished.

The next case dates from about the same year and concerns a teenage girl named Edna, who one sunny Sunday afternoon cycled from her home in the north Wiltshire village of Hannington to visit a friend living in Wanborough. The approximately eight-mile journey took Edna along the old Roman road of Ermine Street, which was then a much quieter road than it is today, and through the village of Stratton St Margaret. By then dark clouds were filling the sky, and as the girl rode along the final stretch of road leading out of Stratton St Margaret thunder sounded and it suddenly began to rain.

Edna, who was in danger of getting drenched, was therefore very relieved to suddenly notice a thatched cottage standing a short way down a side lane, especially as the smoke coming from its chimney revealed there was someone at home. She cycled to the cottage, dismounted, and strode through its neat, well-tended garden to knock on the front door. To her relief the door was quickly and, she noticed, noiselessly opened by a tall, rather odd-looking elderly gentleman with long grey hair and a long grey beard, wearing a dark green waistcoat with bright metal buttons, and smoking a pipe. She hurriedly asked him if she might shelter there from the rain, and the man, after removing his pipe from his mouth, smiled welcomingly at her and beckoned her inside.

Edna stepped gratefully into the cosy, low-ceilinged living-room, which was lit by a wood fire burning in an old-fashioned grate. However she was a little surprised when the man maintained his silence, although he continued to smile at her in his friendly way, and she became aware that it was also completely quiet within the room, despite the fact that a storm was raging outside. Yet no sound of thunder was audible at all!

But what happened next was even more strange, because the next thing Edna (later Mrs Edna Hedges) knew was that she was back on Ermine Street, cycling towards Wanborough. She had no recollection of leaving the cottage or of saying goodbye to its unusual inhabitant. The rain had stopped, and when she reached her friend's house, she was quite dry. This puzzled her friend, who had been worried about her when the storm started and who asked her how she avoided getting wet. Edna explained that she had taken shelter in a cottage, whose location she described. This brought an incredulous gasp from the other girl, who cried out: 'But there isn't a cottage at all on that stretch of road! There's only that derelict one which no one has lived in for half a century!'

One week later, when Edna was able to revisit the lane, she found to her consternation that her friend was right. The cottage in which she had taken shelter was actually a ruined building with broken windows, whose thatched roof was falling in. The rooms all smelled of dampness and decay. Even the neat garden she remembered was overgrown with weeds. And of course there was no sign of the smiling but silent grey-bearded man sporting a green waistcoat with metal buttons.

Two other buildings which have appeared in a similarly mysterious way are described by Elliott O'Donnell in his book *Haunted Britain*, although once again the manifestations were not in fact spectral. Indeed, the couple who saw them, like Edna Hedges, actually went inside one of them, touched its structure, and met its peculiar inhabitants.

One summer two women, says O'Donnell, who were holidaying together at Chagford in Devon, went for a walk on a nearby moor and came across a pair of unusually picturesque cottages. They found them so lovely and so pleasantly situated that they knocked on one of the doors to enquire if there were any rooms to let. The door was answered by a pretty, fair-haired girl, who invited them inside. The furniture of the parlour into which they were admitted was of an antique style, and they could not help but notice a large white cat with very green eyes and a curious-looking black bird in a gilt cage. Then a tall, handsome woman came into the room and told them that unfortunately all the rooms were presently occupied, but that she might have one or two for rent later in the year.

The women went away disappointed, yet it so happened that the following June, having some free time, they returned to the area and purposely searched for the cottages, hoping to find accommodation there. But despite checking every foot of the way they had previously taken, they failed to find them. Quite bewildered by this, they enquired among the locals where the cottages stood, and to their astonishment were told by them that they must have come across the 'vanishing cottages', which only appear on the moor every ten or twelve years!

Both of these occurrences are of great interest, for not only were the cottages entered by the women in question and their reality thus verified by touch as well as by sight, but their inhabitants were also encountered. The cottage interiors were noticeably old-fashioned, and the people living in them and, in the second case, their pets were certainly unusual.

But despite their evident solidity, the cottages and those living in them were not of this world, but had instead seemingly made a temporary supernatural appearance in it. The cottage entered by the young Edna appears to have somehow come from the past. The cottages in Devon might have had a similar origin, or they may have come from another dimension, like the green children of Woolpit, although unlike them they do not get trapped here, but are able to arrive at regular intervals, stay for a limited period, then depart again.

A very similar, but even more remarkable, supernatural appearance happened in October 1979 to four English holiday-makers from Dover, namely bricklayer Len Gisby, 56, his wife Cynthia, and their friends Geoff Simpson, 51, a British Rail employee, and his wife Pauline, while travelling by car through southern France on their way to Spain. After unsuccessfully trying to book into a motel late one evening on the main Montelimar Nord autoroute, they turned off the highway down a tree-lined lane which took them to the village of Cuccolde, where they were relieved to find a picturesque hotel with shuttered windows. They parked their car on the bare patch of ground opposite the hotel and wearily walked across to the olde-worldy but none the less very welcoming establishment. They noticed some circus posters stuck to the wall outside, one of which showed a little man dressed in a leotard, which made Cynthia Gisby comment to her husband, 'My God, that looks ancient!' Entering the hotel, the tall and well-built proprietor, who was rather unusually clad in a collarless white shirt with blue stripes and a pair of thick grey flannel trousers with metal fly-buttons, greeted them in broken English and told them that, yes, but of course he had rooms to rent.

The tired Gisbys and Simpsons booked two double rooms, then ordered a dinner of steak and chips for the men, and egg and chips for the women, which was served to them on heavy old-fashioned plates, while the lager they ordered to accompany it was brought to their table in tankards. Afterwards, they were equally charmed by their bedrooms, which were as old-fashioned as the dining-room and its tableware.

> The beds were so high that you could hardly sit on them, and they had bolsters instead of pillows [Cynthia Gisby told me]. They had thick sheets and several blankets, which were laid over the whole bed and the bolsters. The windows of the room didn't have any glass in them, just the wooden shutters. And the doors didn't have any locks either, but were kept shut by wooden latches. We weren't at all bothered because everything was very nice and, being in rural France, where we had never been before, we just thought that that was the way of life there. And funnily enough, we fell asleep as soon as we lay down and had a very comfortable night that passed in a flash.

Their shared bathroom was likewise antiquated, having as it did a metal bath-tub standing on legs, with a grill at its base upon which one stood to take a shower, while the soap, instead of being in the form of a loose bar, was attached to the bath on an iron rod.

But an even bigger surprise was in store for them the next morning, as when they were eating their breakfast a couple entered the *salle à manger* accompanied by a dog. Although they do not remember much about the man, except that he sported a thin moustache, the woman's long purple-coloured chiffon dress and her button-up boots stuck in their memory, as did the garb of two gendarmes that followed them in and joined them; high hats, gaiters, and black capes, which contrasted oddly with the uniform of the gendarmes the Gisbys and Simpsons had seen during their drive!

Len Gisby took the opportunity of asking the gendarmes, who spoke some English, the way to the autoroute for Avignon, and noted that 'they seemed puzzled at the word "autoroute" and by the word I substituted for it, namely "motorway", but they gave me the directions for Avignon, although they pointed in the opposite direction to which we had come'.

Another surprise came when they paid their bill, which did not total the 250 or so francs that they had expected, but came to only 19 francs! Len and Geoff happily settled up, giving the landlord a 20 franc coin and telling him to keep the change, and then left the hotel with their wives, stopping only to take three photographs of the latter standing in front of the shutters of their bedrooms before continuing their journey south.

The two couples naturally decided that they would take advantage of such cheap and delightful accommodation again on their return from Spain, and when driving back on the Montelimar Nord autoroute they kept a sharp look-out for the same tree-lined lane on which the village of Cuccolde stood. They had no trouble finding the pretty avenue, but to their amazement and consternation the trees lining it seemed bigger than before and the old hotel proved impossible to locate. They drove up and down the lane three times, passing other buildings that they recognized, but neither the hotel nor the bare patch of earth which stood opposite it were anywhere to be seen. Both had, or so it seemed, completely vanished!

'We went to the same Montelimar Nord turn-off, passed the same motel where we had originally asked for accommodation and where we had been advised to try down the road,' insisted a very puzzled Len Gisby. 'We went by the same buildings on the road that we had passed before, and the same advertising signs and the same roadworks sign. We couldn't have been on a different road. In fact everything about the lane was the same, except for the bigger trees and the fact that the old hotel and its lay-by weren't there any more.'

But the mystery did not end there. On their return to Dover the couples sent off their respective rolls of holiday snaps to have them developed. When the prints were posted back, every photograph had come out perfectly – except the ones taken of the women outside the old hotel. Not only were they missing, but the film itself contained no negatives of those photographs! Indeed, it was as if the snaps themselves had never been taken.

This strange but true story suggests that the Gisbys and the Simpsons checked into a hotel that had supernaturally appeared from an earlier age – the clothes worn by the people they met and the furnishings and objects they encountered have been dated to the first decade of this century – and which had managed to maintain itself here during the several hours of the couples' stay. But if so, one wonders what would have happened if they had delayed their departure, or been tempted to stay at such cheap accommodation for another night. They might have vanished with the hotel, perhaps to find themselves taken to the time and place from which it had apparently come.

The two couples were taken back to the village of Cuccolde by

Yorkshire Television in 1983, following the account of their adventure published by the *Dorset Express*, but despite another careful search were still unable to find the hotel at which they had stayed, although they did discover the foundations of a building that had once stood there and which may have been the remains of the hotel. Yet no records have yet been uncovered to verify this.

I asked Mrs Gisby if the hotel's landlord had queried the modern 20 franc coin her husband had given him to pay for their night's lodging, but she said that he accepted it without question. This is the only feature of their story which sounds suspicious, although for all I know a modern, but perhaps worn, 20 franc coin may be virtually indistinguishable from one minted *c.* 1905. If so, then there would be no reason for the landlord to scrutinize the coin's date.

It is relevant to note that many folktales make mention of buildings or other structures that either appear from out of nowhere or are transferred from one place to another. For example, the Dibble Bridge over the River Dibb in Thorpe, North Yorkshire, is said to have supernaturally appeared many years ago following a local shoemaker's encounter with the Devil (which is why the bridge is alternatively known as the Devil's Bridge); and on 10 August 1291, the chapel of Loretto, which stands near the town of Ancon in Italy, was brought by angels, according to local legend, all the way from Judaea in the Middle East.

These and other such legendary appearances may not be true, although the stories themselves could be based on actual events, so that we are hearing echoes of past supernatural happenings, all of which further suggests that our world is not the internally changing yet fixed system it appears to be, wherein everything is kept running by inflexible natural laws, but is in reality far less rigid and predictable than we have thus far dared to imagine.

4　Bilocation

On another occasion another member of the House, Dr Mark Macdonnell, was seen by fellow members on two consecutive days, and actually recorded his vote in the division lobby, though as a matter of fact he had not left his room, being laid up at the time.

From *The Mystery of the Human Double* by Ralph Shirley

The term 'bilocation' means the ability to be in two places at the same time. The phenomenon entails, in other words, a replication of the human form, the two portions of which may become widely separated from one another, so that the copy is sometimes able to visit distant regions, into which it is somehow projected and from which it later supernaturally disappears. The created double can of course be seen by others, and frequently both speaks in a voice, and performs actions, identical to those of the real person. The clothes it wears are likewise replicas of the originals.

People who have seen a double frequently testify that although it often has an unhealthy pallor, it cannot be otherwise distinguished from the real individual, and indeed it is thought to be that person until it either vanishes before their eyes or the subject gives proof that he or she was in another place when the visitation occurred. However, the evidence suggests that the double or *alter ego* is not a full physical replica of the person concerned, but rather is formed of a material that, while genuine enough to the eye, lacks the intrinsic solidity and permanence of normal matter. This is no doubt why the double can only exist for a relatively short time, and hence cannot take up an independent existence of its own.

Bilocation most often occurs when the subject is in a trance, one brought on by meditation or by contemplation, which may explain why the phenomenon is typically associated with saints, hermits, lamas, and other holy men and women, although these are by no means the only ones to whom it happens. A trance state also allows the consciousness of the person replicated to be transferred to the double, thereby enabling it to function as if it really was that person. But when duplication happens to someone who is conscious, such a mind-shift cannot normally take place, which results in a lack of self-awareness and an inability to cogitate by the *alter ego*.

Bilocation is one of the many miracles said to have been performed by St Anthony of Padua. This Portuguese Franciscan monk, who was renowned for his learning and for his skill as a preacher (which was sublime enough to convert criminals and heretics), was conducting a service on Holy Thursday, 1226, at the church of St Pierre du Queyrrix at Limoges, when he suddenly realized that he had promised to attend the service at the monastery chapel on the other side of the town. He gathered his thoughts, knelt down and pulled the hood of his habit over his head, then prayed and remained motionless for some time. After the service was over, word came that he had indeed been at the chapel, his double having miraculously appeared there. In this form he read the lesson and the appointed office, then disappeared, to the astonishment and wonder of the congregation of monks.

Another isolated bilocation was reported of St Alphonsus Liguori (1697–1787), the Italian theologian and founder of the Redemptorists, a group of priests who carried out missionary work in rural areas. He was made bishop of the diocese of Sant' Agata dei Goti in 1762, which while small in size gave him continual administrative and congregational problems, these contributing to the ill-health he experienced during the last twenty years of his life.

In 1774, during one period of sickness, which was aggravated by his habit of fasting, St Alphonsus remained in his cell for five days in a coma-like trance. When he eventually recovered, he told his aides that he had been present at the death bed of Pope Clement XIV in Rome, a journey of some four days away. They of course looked somewhat askance at this, assuming that he must have been suffering from delusions. Yet word eventually came from

Rome that he had been seen by witnesses among the crowd of mourners standing around the dying Pope's bedside, some of whom had both touched and spoken with him.

Such duplication is also said to have happened to several other Catholic saints, including St Ambrose, St Severus of Ravenna, St Clement of Rome, and St Francis Xavier.

Yet while these individual bilocations are certainly remarkable, they cannot compare with those accomplished by the Venerable Mary of Jesus of Agreda, the Spanish nun whose duplicate form repeatedly materialized before hundreds of witnesses on the other side of the Atlantic Ocean, over 2,000 miles away.

Mary Coronel was born at Agreda, in Castile, Spain, on 2 April 1602, the eldest of the two surviving daughters born to Francisco and Cathalina d'Arana Coronel. She was evidently a sensitive and religiously precocious child, who suffered much from various ailments, some doubtless psychological in nature, and from the strict upbringing imposed on her by her parents. From time to time she heard disembodied voices addressing her, one of which spoke with some regularity after her mother had made a small oratory for her. She called the voice her Pole Star and one day it said to her, 'My spouse, turn thyself to me, and forsake that which is earthly and momentary. Rise up, my dove, and flee to me.' This heavenly command prompted the young Mary to make a vow that she would become a nun, which she did by entering the Agreda convent.

In 1620, during one of her ecstatic trances or raptures, Mary had a vision of all the peoples of the world and she noted with dismay that very few of them were Roman Catholics, her attention being particularly taken by the heathen Jumano Indians of New Mexico, an area which had recently been colonized by Spain. Her concern for them led her to pray fervently for their conversion, little realizing that she herself would be responsible for it. For not long afterwards, according to Michael Geddes, one of her early biographers, she had another rapture

in which she found herself in a new region, and in a different climate, and amidst those very Indians she prayed for so particularly. She did very sensibly perceive the great heat of that climate, and observed all its other diversities; she was then commanded to pour out her charity on the Indians she had prayed for so much, by preaching the Christian faith to them. Mary did so, and tho' she spoke to them in Spanish, she was perfectly understood by them, and so was their language by her. But when she came out of her rapture, she found herself in the same place it had seized her in.

This was the first of approximately 500 bilocations that Mary underwent between 1620 and 1631, when she 'did convert the king of that vast country and all his subjects, which were numberless, to the Christian faith'. For she did not, as perhaps might at first be thought, vanish from Agreda and materialize in New Mexico, but rather her normal self remained in Agreda in an ecstatic trance, as was testified by her fellow nuns, while her duplicate miraculously appeared in that distant country, thereby enabling her to successfully carry out her missionary duties. Mary came among the Jumanos clad in a replica of her blue Franciscan habit, and curiously, on one occasion she was able to take with her and distribute numerous rosaries which had been lying in her cell, and which were never seen again afterwards by anyone at the convent.

Mary's miraculous appearances (and disappearances) among the New Mexico Indians came to light when, intent on following her instructions to be baptized, a group of Jumanos went to the nearest Franciscan outpost, situated over 100 miles away, and asked the friars to return with them and perform this important and much desired task. The friars were naturally amazed to discover that the Jumanos had any knowledge of Christianity, let alone the deep understanding which they revealed, and their amazement turned to wonder when, having enquired of the Jumanos who had brought the word of Christ to them, they were informed that it was brought

by a woman, but they could not tell who she was nor from whence she came but they gave an account of the clothes she wore, and of her countenance. The friars perceiving plainly, that her clothes were exactly the habit of the Franciscan nuns, one of them, who happened to have a small picture of Mother Luisa de Carion, a famous Franciscan nun in Spain at that time, for Mary's fame, nor picture, had not yet reach'd those remote parts, he shewed it to the Indians, and asked them whether that was not the woman that had instructed and converted them: they said, the habit was exactly the same, but the face was not, for the woman by whom they were taught, was both much younger, and much handsomer.

The friars' superior Father Alonso de Benavides, suspecting a miracle had taken place, resolved to discover who this remarkable woman was, and apparently concluded, his local enquiries having proved fruitless, that she must live in Spain.

Yet it was not until 1630 that Father Benavides was able to visit Madrid, where he met with the head of the Franciscan Order, who, knowing of Mary of Jesus of Agreda, opined that it was probably her. Father Benavides then travelled secretly to Agreda, where he interviewed Mary about the conversion of the Jumanos. She told him the part she had played in it, giving him by way of proof of her visits

the true names of them all, and did give an exact description of them, and of the habits and military arms of those Indians. In her voyages to New Mexico, she had seen prodigious seas and vast tracts of land, of all which she gave a perfect account: she had been in some of them by day, and in others by night; in some of them she had met with fair weather, and in others with rain; and had seen the Indians on their knees to her praying for a remedy.

It was her accurate accounts of the Jumanos' way of life, about which she could not have known anything without visiting them, for they were a distant and previously uncontacted tribe, which persuaded Father Benavides that she was the woman whom the Jumanos called the 'Lady in Blue'.

Mary's bilocations ended the following year (although Geddes says, wrongly, that they did so in 1623), when the unwelcome celebrity resulting from them, which conflicted with her vows of humility, prompted her to pray for them to stop, a divine dispensation that was evidently granted. She remained at the Agreda convent, however, and became in due course its Abbess, a post which she held, with one short interruption, until her death in 1665. As Abbess she was instrumental in raising funds to have a new convent and church built, and she also wrote a lengthy biography of the Virgin Mary, which she claimed was dictated to her by the Mother of God.

Mary of Jesus of Agreda's bilocations are undoubtedly the most remarkable of their type on record. Her testimony was investigated fully by the Franciscan commissary, her confessor, and a provincial of the order, as well as by Father Benavides, to whom, following the receipt of a letter from the head of the Franciscan Order instructing her to reveal all, she gave the detailed account outlined above of her miraculous travels. It was they who concluded that she must have been physically present in New Mexico; that she had, in other words, duplicated herself, which went against Mary's own judgement of what had happened, for she doubted that she had done so, preferring to think, in her humility, that she had been there only in spirit.

Each of Mary's ecstatic trances, during which her double appeared in New Mexico, lasted no more than three hours, which perhaps explains why so many of them – about 500 – were necessary, especially as some were of a far shorter duration. Her sudden appearances among the Indians, the shortness of her visits, and her equally sudden disappearances, would have been deeply impressive to them, miraculous as they seemed, and must have encouraged them to listen to her words and to adopt her faith. Yet none the less, it is very difficult to comprehend how she was understood by the Jumanos when she spoke to them in Spanish, or how she understood their native tongue. The solution might be that her double was able to read the thoughts of talking Jumanos, while she was able to telepathically channel her thoughts into their minds. In this way a direct mind-to-mind link would operate when one or other of them was speaking, which would enable a seeming comprehension of the spoken words.

The other famous, and more recent, example of bilocation also involved a woman, who similarly duplicated herself on many occasions, yet her case is different in several respects from that of Mary of Agreda. An examination of its main features will help us to throw further light on this puzzling phenomenon.

The woman's name was Emilie Sagée. She was French by birth and a schoolmistress by profession, and we have a record of her curious duplications at the time when she was teaching at the Pensionnat de Neuwelcke, a small school for daughters of the nobility standing a mile and a half outside the town of Wolmar, near Riga, in modern Latvia. She was then about thirty-two years of age. Her case was first reported in the 18 August 1883 issue of *Light* magazine under the title 'Habitual Apparition of a Living

Person'. The author is anonymous, although she says that she obtained her information directly from Mademoiselle Julie de Guldenstubbe, who was one of the pupils at Neuwelcke during the eighteen months (1845-1846) that Mademoiselle Sagée worked there.

Blonde and blue-eyed, Mademoiselle Sagée evidently had a pleasant and generally cheerful, if somewhat nervous, disposition. She was bright and well-educated, and her talents as a teacher were above average. Indeed, she was well liked by her pupils.

But she had not been at the school for many weeks before the girls, of whom there were forty-two, began disagreeing about her whereabouts. One pupil would comment, for example, that she had just seen her in the library, while another, having come from the music room, would protest that that was impossible, as she had been with Mademoiselle Sagée in there. When this strange disparity was repeated on several occasions, it began to alarm the girls, who brought it to the attention of the other teachers. They, however, said it was impossible for someone to be in two places at the same time, and that the girls were therefore mistaken.

Yet the girls' suspicions were entirely substantiated when Mademoiselle Sagée was one day writing on the blackboard in front of a class. To the astonishment and terror of her pupils, a second Mademoiselle Sagée suddenly appeared as if by magic beside her, dressed in identical clothes, and mimicking her actions, although not having any chalk, the double was unable to actually write anything on the board. The resulting screams had the mistress turning quickly around, breathless and red-faced, to quieten her charges, an action that led to the disappearance of her *alter ego*. Yet despite telling them that they had imagined it, the flustered teacher found it impossible to persuade the thirteen girls in the class that they had not seen two of her.

Soon after [continues the anonymous author], one of the pupils, Mademoiselle Antonie de Wrangel, having obtained permission, with some others, to attend a *fête champêtre* in the neighbourhood, and being engaged in completing her toilet, Mademoiselle Sagée had good-naturedly volunteered her aid, and was hooking her dress from behind. The young lady, happening to turn around and to look in an adjacent mirror, perceived two Mademoiselle Sagées hooking her dress. The sudden apparition produced so much effect on her that she fainted.

But Mademoiselle Sagée's double by no means only imitated the actions of the real person, as the following extract makes clear:

Sometimes, when the latter rose from a chair, the figure would appear seated on it. On one occasion, Mademoiselle Sagée being confined to bed with an attack of the influenza, the young lady already mentioned, Mademoiselle de Wrangel, was sitting by her bedside, reading to her. Suddenly the governess became stiff and pale; and, seeming as if about to faint, the young lady, alarmed, asked her if she was worse. She replied that she was not, but in a very feeble and languid voice. A few seconds later, Mademoiselle de Wrangel, happening to look around, saw, quite distinctly, the figure of the governess walking up and down the apartment.

Not long afterwards, the pupils were doing embroidery in one of the large downstairs' rooms, which had four French windows looking out on the garden. They were seated around a long table, and were supervised by another teacher who sat at its head. While they were thus engaged, the girls noticed Mademoiselle Sagée come into the garden and begin picking flowers, which she did with her customary brightness and energy. Their supervisor then rose and, excusing herself, left the room.

The girls continued working while watching Mademoiselle Sagée outside, until one of them, happening to look around, noticed with a shriek that another Mademoiselle Sagée sat in the chair so recently vacated by her colleague! General astonishment followed, with everyone in the room alternately turning to look open-mouthed at the double, then back at the Emilie Sagée who was picking flowers. The two were identical, although the one in the garden, the girls saw, was now moving about slowly and lackadaisically, as if she was lost in another world. Finally, two of the girls, who were bolder than the rest, went up to the double and touched it.

They averred that they did feel a slight resistance, which they likened to that which a fabric of fine muslin or crape would offer to the touch. One of the two passed close in front of the armchair, and actually through a portion of the figure. The appearance, however, remained, after she had done so, for some time longer, still seated, as before. At last it gradually vanished ....

The real Mademoiselle Sagée in the garden then became more animated, and resumed picking flowers with her previous zest.

When she was later questioned by some of the girls about her replication, Mademoiselle Sagée could only say that she had noticed the absence of her colleague in the room and had thought that it might lead to them neglecting their work.

The phenomenon continued, under various modifications, throughout the whole time that Mademoiselle Sagée retained her situation at Neuwelcke; that is throughout a portion of the years 1845 and 1846; and, in all, for about a year and a half; at intervals, however, – sometimes intermitting for a week, sometimes for several weeks at a time. It seemed chiefly to present itself when the lady was very earnest or eager in what she was about. It was uniformly remarked that the more distinct and material to the sight the double was, the more stiff and languid was the living person; and in proportion as the double faded did the real individual resume her powers. She herself, however, was totally unconscious of the phenomenon; she had first become aware of it only from the report of others; and she usually detected it by the looks of the persons present. She never, herself, saw the appearance, nor seemed to notice the species of rigid apathy which crept over her at the times it was seen by others.

Mademoiselle Sagée's double was a spontaneous phenomenon, unwanted and unwilled, and the fact that the woman herself was unable to see it must have been very frustrating to her, particularly as its appearance caused her endless professional difficulties. Indeed, when she was later (and regretfully) sacked from the Pensionnat de Neuwelcke because worried parents, who had heard about the phenomenon from their daughters, started taking them away from the school, she revealed that she had already been dismissed from eighteen other schools for the same reason!

This case is undoubtedly one of the most remarkable of its kind. However, it differs from that of Mary of Agreda in that, being spontaneous, Mademoiselle Sagée's consciousness did not transfer itself into her double and because the double never strayed far from Mademoiselle Sagée:

> During the eighteen months throughout which my informant had an opportunity of witnessing this phenomenon and hearing of it through others, no example came to her knowledge of the appearance of the figure at any considerable distance – as of several miles – from the real person. Sometimes it appeared, but not far off, during their walks in the neighbourhood; more frequently, however, within doors. Every servant in the house had seen it. It was, apparently, perceptible to all persons, without distinctions of age or sex.

Yet when the double arises from someone who is in a trance or a meditative state, the consciousness can be transferred to it, which enables it to not only become self-aware but to cogitate and speak and to perform actions as if it was the real person. In a mental sense, if not wholly in a physical sense, it therefore becomes that person, which allows the subject, like the 'Lady in Blue' in distant New Mexico, to do what he or she could not do ordinarily.

The French explorer Alexandra David-Neel (1869–1968) spent a total of fourteen years travelling in Tibet during the early years of the twentieth century, where she was able to observe and record many of the Buddhist and occult practices of that country's remarkable people. Her meetings with lamas and hermits revealed to her that many of them developed supernatural powers, even though they themselves did not regard them as supernatural. Rather, they believed that such powers derived from the control of ordinary, but little known, energies.

The Tibetans likewise believe in the double or duplicate self, which they hold can, in certain circumstances, separate itself from the physical body. The double may leave the physical body spontaneously (as happened with Emilie Sagée), yet those adepts who acquire the necessary powers of concentration can bring it about at will. The double may then reveal itself, if desired, in distant locations. This technique has important practical applications, as the double may sometimes be sent ahead of a traveller, for example, to alert his hosts of his approach or to assure them that he is well, while at times of grave personal danger the double may save his life by luring pursuers into taking the wrong direction, so allowing him to make his escape.

In her book *Magic and Mystery in Tibet* (1929), Alexandra David-Neel relates how the double of her distant and long-overdue servant named Wangdu appeared ahead of him. She was prompted to look out for the young man by a dream she had had the previous night:

> The place where I stood dominated a valley. I distinctly saw Wangdu. He was dressed exactly as I had seen him in my dream. He was alone and walking slowly up the path that wound up the hill slope.
>
> I remarked that he had no luggage with him and the servant who was next to me answered: 'Wangdu has walked ahead, the load-carriers must be following.'
>
> We both continued to observe the man. He reached a small chorten [or monument made of stones], walked behind it and did not reappear ... as time went by without his reappearing, I inspected the ground round the monument with my field-glasses, but discovered nobody.
>
> Very much puzzled I sent two of my servants to search for the boy. I followed their movements with the glasses but no trace was to be found of Wangdu nor of anybody else.
>
> That same day a little before dusk the young man appeared in the valley with his caravan. He wore the very same dress and the foreign sun hat whch I had seen in my dream, and in the morning vision.

Alexandra David-Neel immediately and separately interrogated Wangdu and his companions about where they had spent the night, and learned that it was not only at a place so distant that none could have reached the chorten by daybreak, but that the party had remained together throughout their journey.

Hence the real Wangdu had not come ahead. Rather, his double had, and had thereby given Alexandra David-Neel notice of the real Wangdu and his party's imminent return. The double was not a subjective 'vision', for it was seen by both her and at least one other servant. However, Alexandra David-Neel suggests that the double was a spontaneous manifestation and so had not been consciously willed to appear by Wangdu.

A spontaneous duplication may on occasion be brought about by a person wishing himself to be where he is not, such as might happen, for example, if he is stuck in a traffic jam and yearns to be at home. The following appearance of such a double was witnessed by my aunt, Peggy Sullivan, who was kind enough to describe what she saw for me. Her account demonstrates that such remarkable events are happening to ordinary people today, and also that a double originating from someone who is conscious may exhibit more awareness and mentality than is perhaps usual.

> One day in the mid-1980s [she writes], I had performed my usual weekday afternoon chores, which were to walk and feed the dogs, prepare our evening meal and lay the table. Then, again as usual, I put my feet up in the chair by the lounge window, and dozed. I awoke to hear my partner's voice, 'I'm home, dear,' and saw him crossing the room towards me. He came over to my chair, and bent and kissed me, saying, 'Oh, that journey! Won't I be glad when I retire!' He had to make the return journey from work in the rush hour each weekday evening, usually reaching home between six and 6.30, and he loathed being stuck in the traffic jams, especially in the summer.
>
> I jumped up quite flustered. 'Goodness, I didn't know it was that late!' I exclaimed. 'You go and get changed. I'll put the oven on and pour you a drink.' I attended to these things and called out, 'Your drink's poured.' After about five minutes and hearing nothing, I looked in the bedroom and bathroom, but he was not to be seen, so I thought he had gone back out to the car for something. I went outside, but there was no car in the drive or garage. Then, for no explainable reason, I looked at the clock. The time said 5.40 – at least twenty minutes before he could possibly arrive back. He was not at home. He eventually came home at 6.15.

My aunt remarked that she woke to see her ersatz partner at about 5.30 p.m., when he was in reality encountering the first heavy traffic on his drive home, and that he appeared entirely life-like and normal. She definitely felt his kiss on her cheek, which suggests, interestingly, that his double had a discernible solidity. She rose from her chair when he turned from her, so that she saw his back view as he left the room. It was only later she realized that their two dogs had not come frisking into the room with him as they usually did. However, on going out to the kitchen she found them waiting in the hall for him, where they usually sat, although she thought at the time that they were waiting for him to come out of the bedroom.

The appearance of the double in this case has some unique features, the most important being that the man from whom it originated, Peggy's partner Nigel, was quite conscious when it manifested (he was driving a car), and that unlike the duplicate of Mademoiselle Sagée his double was able to speak and respond to Peggy's suggestions. It also appeared some miles away from the real Nigel. And then, having left the room apparently to get changed, it completely disappeared. The manifestation was brief, went unnoticed by the couple's dogs, and served no apparent purpose. Nigel says that he was not specifically thinking of Peggy at the time, which suggests that his double was spontaneously generated by his desire or wish to be out of the traffic and at home. Thus you can, it seems, really be in two places at the same time!

The generation of a duplicate, whether consciously or unconsciously, has similarities to, but also differences from, the phenomenon known as astral projection. The latter is the name given to the exteriorization of the astral or etheric (= spiritual) body from the physical body, which may allow it to visit distant sites. Astral projection can either occur spontaneously, as it may, for example, when someone is asleep, or it can be self-induced. It is always accompanied by a separation of the consciousness from the physical body, which has led some researchers to suggest that astral travel is really mind/body separation and not the splitting of some mysterious spiritual component, which incorporates the mind, from the body.

The astral body, unlike the double, is normally quite invisible to others, although it can on occasion be seen. Its perceived form, by the person to whom it happens, also varies. One astral traveller may report that he still had his human shape, whereas another will say that his shape was quite different, with various geometric forms or even points of light being among the commoner alternatives. The double, by contrast, is always, as its name suggests, a duplicate of the real person, and it is always visible to others.

The astral body can easily penetrate matter and so pass unhindered through walls and doors, which suggests that it is entirely non-physical, whereas the double has a degree of physicality and thus cannot behave like a ghost, despite being able to appear supernaturally out of thin air and to vanish in an equally astonishing way. Most astral travellers also report that they cannot communicate with others while out of the body or affect their environment in any way, yet the conscious duplicate is not so circumscribed. It is able to have conversations with those around it and it can move or otherwise manipulate solid objects. The double is therefore a three-dimensional entity in its own right, whereas the astral body, although conscious, is not.

The composition of the double is as yet a mystery. The phenomenon, quite simply, is so rare that no sample has been taken from a double's 'body' and analysed. However, it may be that the gauze-like extrusion known as ectoplasm, which is produced by trance mediums and which can, on occasion, organize itself into human-like 'spirit forms', has the same, or a related, structure. Ectoplasm is a physical substance, yet unusually light in weight, and microscopic examination of it appears to show a cellular organization. It is usually extruded from the mouth, the nose, and/or other orifices of the medium's body. But while it seems to be a suitable substrate from which the double might be formed, the fact remains that no extruded ecotplasm has ever, at least as far as I know, organized itself into a double of the medium from which it comes, whereas we might suppose that it would naturally tend to assume his or her form.

In this respect it is interesting to note that whereas most modern religions maintain that our physical bodies are inhabited by immaterial souls, which gives no basis for the production of a semi-physical replica, certain pagan peoples had a very different view of our inner structure. Both the ancient Germans and Scandinavians, for example, believed that the soul or second 'ego' could leave the body and take up a semi-independent existence, either as a double of the person or in an animal form, that it was partly physical in composition, and that it could function in much the same way as the person or the animal type into which it manifested. The Scandinavians referred to it as the *fylgia*, which means 'the follower' or 'the second'. The fylgia could be injured or even killed, the injury it suffered simultaneously affecting the real person, while its death resulted in his or her death as well.

Although the astral body can be willed to leave the physical body, its separation usually occurs spontaneously, if at all, and then, typically, only once in a person's lifetime. Such may also be true of the double. But because duplication is rarely partnered by a transfer of consciousness, and because the double is often (but not always) invisible to the person from whom it originates, then he or she will only know of its generation when told by others that it has been seen. This is particularly true of those cases where the double appears at a distant place.

Another interesting example of such a 'one-off' duplication happened to a young married woman named Henrietta Pigott-Carleton in September 1873. At the time she was holidaying with her husband at her father's shooting lodge in County Tyrone. A family friend, Captain M., was also staying with them, and on the day in question Mrs Pigott-Carleton accompanied the captain when he went fishing in the nearby river. 'My husband had some engagement, but my father walked a short way with us,' she writes. 'He never cared to have me long away from him, and, upon turning back, remarked, as he left me, "Don't get too far from home".'

The pair, none the less, walked about four miles along the river-bank before the captain stopped to fish and Mrs Pigott-Carleton sat down to read the novel she had brought with her. All seemed perfect until, suddenly glancing up, the lady caught sight of an advancing storm cloud.

> I saw we were in for a drenching, thought how it would fidget my father, and wished myself back at home with all my heart. In a few minutes the storm burst upon us. Shelter there was next to none, and as soon as the deluge had somewhat abated we made for the lodge, looking as though we had barely escaped from a watery grave.

Captain M. and Mrs Pigott-Carleton had almost reached the lodge, when they were suddenly and unexpectedly met by a search party consisting of the lady's father, her husband, and several employees of the former, which surprised and puzzled her. Her feelings turned to annoyance when her father next berated her for 'foolhardiness', and on returning with them to the lodge she retired to her room, somewhat angry.

> The next day [she continues], I boldly entered upon the subject with my father, hoping free discussion might help to disperse his disquietude. He told me that some little time after his return from the river, he sat down to read, with his back to the (western) window; that suddenly *a shadow fell across the page* [author's italics]; that, turning his head, he

saw me standing at the half-open window, my arms resting upon the push-down sash; that he said, 'Halloa! Back already!'; that I made no reply, but apparently stepped down off the low outer window sill and disappeared; that he put a mark in his book, got up, and looked out of the window; that, not seeing me, he first went to the servants and asked if I had come in at the back door; and then went out on to the little terrace before the lodge and looked around for me; that he suddenly caught sight of the coming storm cloud; that his bewilderment changed to uneasiness, and that my husband just then coming in they speedily started a search.

Mrs Pigott-Carleton perhaps rightly surmises that the appearance of her double was caused by her wishing 'with all her heart' to be at home, while its objectivity and 'solidity' seem to be assured by the fact that it cast a shadow. She had, of course, no idea that she had generated a double until told that she had, yet the distance – four miles – that it manifested from her is considerably greater than those achieved by the double of Emilie Sagée, although this was probably because Mademoiselle Sagée had no desire or need to be elsewhere at those times.

However, the double's apparent inability to attain full physicality is partly belied by the story told of the French knight Walter of Bierbeeke (who flourished *c.* AD 1200), a relative of Henry, Duke of Louvain, whose double is said to have jousted with great success in a tournament while he stopped *en route* to the event to say mass in a chapel. If true, it suggests that on certain exceptional occasions the double can achieve a solidity equal to that of the human body. This may even have happened in the case of Nigel mentioned earlier.

It is usual for those who have achieved astral separation, like those who have had a near death experience, to see their comatose physical body and the surrounding environment before moving away from them, as may happen, to another place. The opposite is sometimes encountered with the phenomenon of the double, whereby the person from whom it manifests may see it and thus seemingly his own self. Such an apparition is described by William Wordsworth in his poem *Peter Bell, A Tale*:

Close by a brake of flowering furze
(Above it shivering aspens play)

He sees an unsubstantial creature,
His very self in form and feature,
Not four yards from the broad highway.

This is, hardly surprisingly, a disturbing experience for those to whom it happens and one that has over the years acquired a dreadful reputation, being said to augur the death of the person concerned. There are certainly cases on record when such a premonition came true, to the extent of death immediately following, such as happened to the French Foreign Legionnaire described by the writer Wellesley Tudor Pole, who

> when seemingly beyond speech, he half rose from the pillow in the sand where he had tried to take refuge from the sun, and cried out in broken French (I translate), 'Why, there is myself coming to meet me. How wonderful!' Then he fell back and died and we reported the incident on reaching Bou Saada the next day.

However, seeing one's self in this way does not invariably mean imminent death (as it did not for Peter Bell!). The German poet Wolfgang Goethe (1749–1832) once saw his own double while out riding, yet oddly it was not his exact duplicate as it wore clothes of a different style and cut to his own. Goethe did not die, as he had perhaps feared, although some eight years later, while out for another ride, he suddenly realized that he was travelling along the same path and in the same direction as his double and that he was wearing identical clothes, although 'not from choice but by accident'.

He had thus seen his double in the guise of himself in the future!

5   Animal Entrances and Exits

'Now open your eyes', said the man, 'and tell me, before you open your hand, what there is in it.'
'A halfpenny in mine,' said Tim.
'A guinea in mine,' replied I.
We opened our hands, and they were empty.

From *Japhet, In Search of a Father* by Captain Marryat

The remarkable phenomenon of the supernatural disappearance and the subsequent materialization of the disappearant, if this occurs, is not confined to members of our species. Other creatures can also vanish and reappear in this way from time to time, just as inanimate objects can.

There are, for example, several supernatural animal appearances recounted in Greek mythology, the best known of which is the winged ram that materialized as Phrixus was about to be sacrificed by his father Athamas, and on whose back Phrixus and his sister Helle made their escape. But perhaps more interesting is the physical disappearance of Iphigenia, King Agamemnon's daughter, as she was about to be sacrificed at Aulis (in 1198 BC), and her miraculous replacement, according to some sources, by a large and beautiful goat, or as others say, by either a hind or a she-bear. And Roman legend tells us of the virgin Metella, who was carried off, as she was about to be sacrificed by her father, by the goddess Vesta, who replaced her with a heifer.

Greek myth also mentions that Zeus manifested as a snow-white bull to ravish the lovely maiden Europe, and as a white swan to mate with Nemesis (or Leda), who had transformed herself into a wild goose.

English legend includes the miraculous appearance of four white

77

oxen on the village green at Alfriston, East Sussex, in the fourteenth century. The beasts lay down together, it is said, with their hindquarters touching, in the form of a St Andrew's cross (or cross saltire), which was taken as a sign from heaven that a church should be built on the spot. This was done, and the cross-shaped church, which still stands, was dedicated to St Andrew, the patron saint of Scotland.

If such appearances sound too fanciful for words, then it may come as a shock to discover that they are not limited to past times. That is something Derek Steedman, who farms at Chillerton on the Isle of Wight, knows only too well.

One cold morning in January 1984, when he opened his livestock sheds, Farmer Steedman was staggered to find that mixed in with the dozen Hereford calves he had carefully locked in the night before, was an approximately two-week-old white bull calf. It was quietly standing with the Herefords, as if waiting for him, and there was no sign of any forced entry into the building which might have explained its presence among them. The attractive little white bull was later identified as a French Charolais cross-breed, and it had, or so it seemed, simply materialized in the stock shed during the night. Its lack of ear tags or other identifying markings meant its owner could not be determined, if it had ever had one, and Farmer Steedman's attempts to discover who he was came to nothing. It was a puzzling and unsolvable mystery!

But it is perhaps more common for ordinary cattle, and sometimes horses, to be teleported or supernaturally moved from one place to another. Such movements are sometimes associated with properties that are haunted, and the translocated animals may even have to be rescued from somewhere they could not have entered on their own or into which they could not have been led by someone. Indeed, special lifting equipment is sometimes required to free them.

Following the exposure to public view of the mummified body of Miss Beswick at Birchen Bower, Hollinwood, in the nineteenth century (an event which took place every twenty-one years), writer John Graham records that

the horses and the cows were always found let loose, and sometimes a cow would be found up in the hayloft, although how it came there was, indeed, a mystery, as there was no passage large enough to admit a beast of such magnitude ... how the cow got up there was a mystery to everyone, while that blocks had to be borrowed from Bower Mill to let it down through the hay hole outside the barn was an equally well-known fact.

Moving back into the twentieth century Elliott O'Donnell, writing in *Haunted Britain*, mentions that

A curious form of haunting is said to occur at a farm where an atrocious murder was committed. The farm is situated about mid-way between Blackpool and Garstang. Cows that are confined at night in a certain shippon or cowshed are always found in the morning at the end of a field. Attempts to obtain a satisfactory explanation to the happenings on natural grounds have signally failed.

A much more recent and dramatic example of the teleportation of cattle happened in Wales in late 1977. The six instances of cattle movement involved the herd of dairy cows owned by the Coombs family at Ripperstone Farm, which is situated near the village of St Brides on the peninsula south of St Brides Bay, in Dyfed (formerly Pembrokeshire). The events were preceded by UFO activity in the area, which reportedly centred on Ripperstone Farm, and which included the appearance of a strange silver-suited figure at the farm, although nothing similar was witnessed on the days when the teleportations happened. In fact, there is no more reason to link the disappearing cows with alien beings in this case, than there is to associate the moving cows described by Elliott O'Donnell with a horrid murder.

Farmer William (or Billy) Coombs had one hundred cows at the time of the incidents – November 1977 – of which most were older females ready to calve, while the remainder, sixteen in number, were virgin heifers whose first season was expected. This meant that the animals were being carefully watched by Farmer Coombs, who regularly inspected them and the cowsheds where they were housed and padlocked before he went to bed.

There were in fact two cowsheds at Ripperstone Farm, both containing fifty stalls wherein each cow or heifer was separately locked at night. They stood together one hundred yards distant from the farmhouse.

At midnight on the first day on which a calf had been born, Farmer Coombs went to the cowsheds and spent an hour going from stall to stall checking up on each animal. Having satisfied himself that all was well, he was in the process of locking the cows up again when he heard the telephone ringing at the farmhouse. He quickly returned to answer it and found that his caller was a neighbour named Martin Chambers, who lived half a mile away at Dale Farm. To Coombs's astonishment Chambers told him that his cows were at his farm wandering around loose outside the cowsheds and would he please come and get them. Coombs protested that they couldn't possibly be his cows, but Chambers was adamant that they were, as they all had his yellow and green marker tags attached to their ears. Putting down the phone, Billy Coombs hurried back to his cowsheds to assure himself that his cows were where he had left them, but was absolutely staggered to discover that all the animals had disappeared. They were, in fact, as Martin Chambers had said, all down at Dale Farm!

The incident is made more puzzling by Martin Chambers's claim that he had first noticed the Coombs's herd at his farm at midnight, and that he had spent the next hour trying unsuccessfully to get through to Ripperstone Farm by telephone to report its unwonted presence. But it was not until one o'clock in the morning that the telephone was answered, which is when Billy Coombs first heard it ringing. This suggests either that Farmer Coombs, for whatever reason, deliberately and maliciously herded his cows down to Dale Farm just before midnight, although this would have been virtually impossible for him to do on his own in the dark, or that some odd and inexplicable dislocation of time took place between the two farms to accompany the genuine teleportation of the animals from one to the other.

However, we might perhaps be tempted to opt for the first explanation had not the cows disappeared and reappeared on other occasions. Two days later, for instance, Billy Coombs checked the cows last thing at night and made sure that each was locked in its own stall, yet in the morning he discovered that one stall was empty and that the animal it had contained was in a nearby stall along with its normal occupant.

Again, one morning some days later Farmer Coombs went to the cattle sheds with his son Clinton and asked him to herd all the heifers into one of the two fenced paddocks while he picked up some hay bales to feed them with. When this had been done and the heifers had been given the hay, the two men went into the dairy to prepare for milking the other animals. But then, on suddenly looking back into the paddock, they discovered to their complete amazement that the heifers had vanished, and on running out to see what had happened to them, they found them, agitated and upset, in the second paddock!

But the most astounding disappearance and reappearance happened not long afterwards when Billy Coombs was visited by Norfolk farmer and UFO expert Paul Palmer and his fiancée Janet, who served as independent witnesses to them. On the morning after their arrival Farmer Coombs took the pair to the cowsheds and enlisted their help in moving the cows into the larger paddock and the heifers into the smaller one, wherein they were locked. Billy then took Paul and Janet into one of the cowsheds to show them a new-born calf. Yet when they emerged a few minutes later they found both of the locked paddocks quite empty of animals, which had unaccountably disappeared. Farmer Coombs then drove with Paul and Janet straight to Dale Farm, thinking that they might be there, only to find that there was no sign of them. He then spent two hours driving around the area looking in vain for his animals, before returning to Dale Farm, where he found his herd outside the farmhouse.

On guiding the animals back to Ripperstone Farm and locking them in the paddocks again, Billy Coombs and his two astonished visitors retired to the farmhouse for lunch, during which time the ground outside received a downpour of rain. Then another telephone call was received from Martin Chambers, who said that the cows were back at his farm! On going to the paddocks, the incredulous trio not only saw that they were empty of cows but could find no sign of fresh hoof marks in the wet and soft ground, which was evidence that the animals had not been released and herded away, impossible though this would have been without detection, by some mysterious third party.

The herd was again returned to the paddocks and carefully locked in, yet ten minutes later they vanished for the third and last time, turning up, to everyone's annoyance and dismay, at Dale Farm!

These supernatural disappearances and reappearances, which is what they genuinely seem to have been, were very stressful to the animals concerned. When found after being transported they were restless and agitated, and their fright stayed with them during the following days; they were readily stampeded when out in a field and would even try to break through barbed wire fences, often injuring themselves, one so badly that she had to be destroyed. The milk yield of the herd decreased, and there was a danger that many of the cows might abort their calves, although I have not been able to determine if any actually did. All in all, it was an experience which the herd neither enjoyed nor would seemingly wish to experience again.

It is a complete mystery as to why these teleportations should suddenly affect the Coombs's herd, for although there had apparently been some UFO activity in the area beforehand there was none, as I said earlier, on the days in question. And anyhow, we have already noted many supernatural disappearances and reappearances that have occurred in the absence of UFOs, which suggests that they are instead a spontaneous phenomenon.

This suggests that we should avoid chuckling up our sleeves when we read about ancient cases of animal appearances like those mentioned earlier, or about the apparent teleportation of horses recorded by Herodotus, the father of history.

Herodotus says that when the Greek hero Heracles was returning from the island of Erytheia with the cattle of Geryon, an expedition known as his Tenth Labour, he journeyed with them into the vastness of Scythia, where, coincidentally, St Andrew is said to have travelled in the latter part of his life. Finding the land largely uninhabited and the weather bitterly cold, Heracles wrapped himself up in his lion skin and went to sleep. And 'while he slept,' records Herodotus, 'the horses which he had unharnessed from his chariot and turned loose to graze mysteriously disappeared.' It was only much later that Heracles found they had been miraculously transported far south to the peninsula of Hylaea or the Woodland, which projects into the Black Sea, where they were in the possession of a viper-woman.

6   Slipping Away in Somerset

The queen would perhaps have accepted it, she had even called a meeting of her great barons to deliberate on the proposition, when, the day before the meeting was to be held, at the moment when Ogier was kneeling at her feet, she perceived a crown of gold which an invisible hand had placed on his brow; and in an instant a cloud enveloped Ogier, and he disappeared for ever from her sight. It was Morgana, the fairy, whose jealousy was awakened at what she beheld, who now resumed her power, and took him away with her in the island of Avalon.

From *Legends of Charlemagne* by Thomas Bulfinch

One of the most famous disappearances, which may even have been supernatural, was that of the Holy Grail, the cup used by Christ at the Last Supper. Legend has it that the Grail was initially kept and treasured by Joseph of Arimathea, the man who buried Christ in his own tomb, and who was afterwards imprisoned for thirty years. On his release Joseph journeyed with the Grail to Gaul, where he met the apostle Philip, who put him in charge of a group of twelve disciples and sent them all across the Channel to convert pagan Britain.

Joseph and his group, who arrived in Britain in 63 AD, first tried to convert King Aviragus, but failed to do so, although the monarch was sufficiently impressed with their beliefs and bearing to grant them twelve hides of land (about 1,440 acres) at Ynys-witrin, or the Isle of Glass, in the west of England, for a religious settlement. There Joseph and his followers built the first Christian church in Britain, which was made of boughs and dedicated to the Virgin Mary. Ynys-witrin was later called Glaestinaburg by the Saxons, and the town which now occupies the site is named Glastonbury. The county in which it stands, and where the Holy Grail may still be hidden, is of course Somerset.

Even today Somerset is an essentially rural and rather mysterious county. Much of it is low-lying, and in the time of Joseph of Arimathea wide areas were either under water, subject to periodic flooding, or marshy. Remains of ancient marsh villages inhabited by Celtic tribes like the Dobunni have been discovered there, although most of the population would have been confined to the Mendip Hills and other upland areas.

But mystery is perhaps to be expected in the county which was home to King Arthur and the knights of the Round Table, and where they went on the quest for the Holy Grail. And somewhere amid Somerset's former misty and marshy waters lay the Isle of Avalon, or the Isle of Apples, to which Arthur was taken after his death.

Nor is it surprising, in view of the wizard Merlin's association with it, that Somerset later became infamous for its witches and magicians, or that the Devil reputedly carried off people from there.

With this in mind, let us first examine two so-called legendary disappearances blamed on the Devil, which form part of Somerset folklore, and then two genuine and startling supernatural disappearances.

There is a cave set in the hills to the north of the market town of Shepton Mallet, in which once lived, it is said, a poor woman named Nancy Camel. One day the Devil, noting her distress and hoping to thereby gain her soul, offered her riches and a life of ease in exchange for it. To Satan's delight, Nancy Camel agreed to this and for the rest of her life, despite continuing to live in the cave, she never worked again and was never in need.

Years later, on the night of Nancy's death, there was a great storm, through which the Devil was reputed to have driven a horse and cart to Nancy's cave to carry her to Hell. Those living close by heard the crack of Satan's whip, the ominous creaking of the cart's wheels, and, soon afterwards, Nancy's shrill screams as she was forced to keep her part of the bargain. The next day worried neighbours who called at the cave found, to their horror, impressions of horses' hooves and cart-wheel tracks in its dank walls, but no sign of poor Nancy Camel, who was never seen again.

Similarly, during the nineteenth century, a ploughboy went to the smithy at Rodhuish village, which stands on the western edge of the Exmoor Forest, to have a broken ploughshare repaired and sharpened. While that was being done, the butcher's boy, who happened to pass by, stopped and got into conversation with him. The two boys talked, among other things, of the horned being named the Croydon Hill Devil that was reputed to live at the top of that hill. In fact their conversation gave the butcher's boy the idea of dressing up in a bullock's hide and pretending to be the Devil, in order to frighten the ploughboy as he walked home. That decided upon, he hurried away to put his plan into action.

Sometime later, as the ploughboy climbed the lane to the top of Croydon Hill, a horned creature suddenly jumped out of the trees in front of him, bellowing like a fiend. In his panic, the ploughboy struck out at the 'monster' with his newly sharpened plough blade, then turned and ran for his life. When he thankfully reached his home in one piece, he gasped out to his fellow villagers what had happened to him, and they immediately went up the hill to see if they could catch the demon. But all they found, so the story goes, was a bullock's hide with a long slash in it. It was only later that they and the ploughboy heard that the butcher's boy was missing, never to be seen again. Word soon went around that he had been taken by the Devil, especially when hideous howls, uttered as if by a soul in torment, began to be heard on Croydon Hill on dark and stormy nights.

Who knows what really happened to Nancy Camel and the anonymous butcher's boy? The tales might be echoes of actual supernatural disappearances, conveniently blamed on the Devil, or the vanishings might be much more mundane. Nancy, for example, might have been murdered and her body hidden by her assailants, while the ploughboy might have delivered a fatal blow to the disguised butcher's boy, who dropped the bullock's hide, staggered back into the undergrowth and there bled to death, his body never to be found. Or the stories may simply be fictions composed by some rustic story-teller, of whom in the old days there were many, but which eventually came to be regarded as actual happenings.

In the 1760s Somerset was a far more rural and out of the way place than it is today, which is borne out by the following contemporary description: 'Somersetshire is a large plentiful sea-county in the west of England, in circumference 204 miles, containing about 907,500 acres; it affords great plenty of excellent corn, and good pasture, which feeds abundance of fine cattle; and also yields plenty of lead, copper, crystal stones, and woad for dyers: its chief manufactures are cloth and serges.'

It was in 1768 that a baffling disappearance took place just outside the town of Shepton Mallet, an incident which is, despite lacking the diabolical accompaniments of Nancy Camel's vanishing, perhaps stranger than Nancy's supposed abduction by the Devil. For not only is it true but it has never been satisfactorily explained.

On the evening of Monday 6 June 1768, not long after six o'clock, retired tailor Owen Parfitt was sitting comfortably in an armchair just outside the front door of his cottage, which stood next to the old toll-road linking Shepton Mallet with Wells, at Wester Shepton, Broad Cross. He was about seventy years of age, of middle height, grey-haired, and a little on the plump side. A passing stranger might have wondered why he was attired in his nightshirt, with a greatcoat placed around his shoulders, whereas a local would have guessed that old Owen was sitting there like that, taking the air and watching the carts go by, because his older but spryer sister, with whom he lived, was taking the opportunity to make his bed and tidy his room. For Owen Parfitt was a cripple, the victim of a stroke and of arthritis, and had been bedridden for several years. Indeed, he could not walk without assistance, and he had been carried downstairs and sat outside by his sister, with the help of their 25-year-old maidservant Susannah Snook.

After Susannah had aided Miss Parfitt in taking Owen outside, she returned upstairs with her to help her make the bed. That done, Susannah left the house, her day's work over, while Miss Parfitt continued tidying her brother's room. Fifteen minutes later the old woman went downstairs again, but not hearing a sound from outside, called out: 'Owen, where are you?' When she did not receive a reply, she put her head out of the front door, and saw, to her alarm, that her brother wasn't there anymore. His chair still stood in the same place – it had his greatcoat laid across it – but of old Owen there was no sign.

Miss Parfitt's shrill cries quickly alerted her neighbours, and hearing the disturbance, Susannah Snook returned immediately to the cottage, where she found the old woman in a nearly hysterical state, crying bitterly and completely confused by the suddenness of her brother's disappearance. Susannah did her best to calm her and then helped her look for Owen Parfitt, doubtlessly thinking that the old chap must be around somewhere. But on the contrary, he was nowhere to be seen, either inside the cottage or outside it. By this time people had gathered to find out what had happened, and they soon spread out to look for the elderly ex-tailor.

The search continued for the rest of the evening and through the night, despite the fact that about one hour afterwards a storm blew up, but those looking did not let the thunder and lightning or the rain deter them. Fields, copses, hedges, outhouses, streams, even the hayricks that were then being erected, all were searched, and wells were probed, a task that went on during the whole of the following day, but without any success. Nothing that might serve as a clue to the whereabouts of Owen Parfitt was found: no dropped handkerchief, no torn piece of clothing, not one scuff mark on the ground, and certainly not the old man, either alive or dead. He had, or so it seemed, vanished completely.

The years then went by, with Miss Parfitt dying not long after her brother's mysterious disappearance. The eighteenth century ended and a new one began, and it seemed as if Owen Parfitt and the mystery of his strange exit from the world would be completely forgotten. And perhaps they might have been, but for the gruesome discovery made by one Henry Strode in 1813, when digging in his garden at Broad Cross, about 150 yards from Owen Parfitt's old home. 'Two feet under the surface of the soil,' reported Strode, 'I dug up a piece of a very old wall and found, at the end of it, a skeleton lying face downwards. It seemed as if the person had been thrown in hastily, after death; for the skeleton lay all in a heap. I picked up the skull.'

It was immediately assumed that the skeleton must surely be that of Owen Parfitt, and a Dr Butler of Shrewsbury, who had long-standing connections with Shepton Mallet, hearing of the find, requested that it be sent to him for further examination. Dr Butler's hopes were evidently high of at long last solving the 45-year-old mystery, and his initial impressions on viewing the skeleton did nothing to dampen his optimism. Yet when he showed it to a surgeon and an anatomist for an expert opinion (for Butler's doctorate was not in medicine), he was told that he could not be more wrong. The skeleton, he was disappointed to learn, did not belong to an old man, but to a young woman!

Yet the discovery of the mystery skeleton and the new interest it aroused in the disappearance of Owen Parfitt, prompted a Shepton Mallet attorney named William Maskell and some other wealthy citizens to hold a public inquest the following year into the affair; they may even have been stimulated to do so by the publicity attendant upon the equally mysterious and apparently unsolvable disappearance of British diplomat Benjamin Bathurst in 1809, an account of which is given in the next chapter. Several of those living in 1768 who either knew Owen Parfitt or had played a part in the search for him were dead, yet the inquiry did turn up a number of useful witnesses, notably the then 71-year-old Susannah Snook, whose testimony provided much of the information about the affair given above.

Some witnesses were able to give an account of Owen Parfitt's early life, but this evidence was intriguingly, but perhaps understandably, inconsistent. Susannah Snook, for instance, who had apparently had many talks with Parfitt while in his employ, said of him, 'He had been in the British Army and had served in Africa,' while another, named Joanna Mills, disagreed with this, saying, 'I was a distant relation of Owen Parfitt. He was neither in the King's service, nor had he any pension. He was wild, and he went away in his youth to Africa and America.' Hence it would seem that Susannah had been given a version of Parfitt's life as he would have liked it to have been, whereas in reality his excursions abroad were not made for king and country but for adventure and profit. In fact there were local rumours, although they were no more than this, that Owen Parfitt had once been a pirate.

One witness, Jehosaphat Stone, claimed that Owen Parfitt's sister, while upstairs, had heard 'a noise' outside, which brought her down to find that her brother had vanished and that the chair in which he had been sitting had been moved. Stone also made the assertion that, 'Many folk round here at the time believed that Owen Parfitt had been spirited off by supernatural means.' However, Susannah Snook was quite adamant that Miss Parfitt had heard no noise and that the chair had not been moved either. These two pieces of second-hand testimony are of course completely at variance and we cannot at this late date know whom to believe, although Susannah Snook was first on the scene and would have heard Miss Parfitt's version of the events uncorrupted by either time or speculation.

The Owen Parfitt mystery is one in which the evidence points towards a possible supernatural disappearance. Owen Parfitt was so incapacitated that he could not have 'picked up his bed and walked'. He might, it is true, have managed to crawl a short way unassisted, but he would certainly have soon been found had he done so. Hence he could not have gone anywhere on his own. However, he had been sitting at the edge of a toll-road, which makes it possible for him to have perhaps been bundled into a passing wagon and driven off, yet nothing was heard by Miss Parfitt to suggest that such a thing happened. An unspecified 'noise' might have been heard, but the sister said nothing about hearing a cry for help or the sound of a wagon and its horses stopping then starting again, or anything similar. And nothing suspicious like that was seen by workers scything hay in the adjacent fields. In fact as far as they were concerned, one moment old Parfitt was sitting in his chair, and the next he was gone. Besides, Owen Parfitt was too poor to be worth robbing, and any serious enemies he might have made while a young buck gadding about the world would surely not have waited until both he and they were seventy years old before abducting him and taking their revenge. In case it might be thought that some neighbour with a grudge was responsible, it is worth remembering that Parfitt, as Susannah Snook told the inquiry, 'could not move at all without aid of someone else, and, when he vanished, had been a cripple for many years'. Thus he was not in any condition, one would have thought, to have upset anyone very much, at least not to the extent of him or them risking a capital charge by kidnapping and murdering him.

The second Somerset disappearance, according to author Colin Parsons who recorded it, brings us forward in time just over two hundred years, to the evening of Sunday 28 July 1974. But the disappearance in question ends far more happily than it did for Owen Parfitt, as the man who vanished in front of several witnesses, Peter Williamson, was returned to the world three days later, puzzled and confused but thankfully safe.

On that evening Peter Williamson and his wife Mary, who had two children, gave a barbecue at their house for a group of friends. The weather had been uncomfortably warm and humid all day, and as people arrived at the Williamson house the sky was turning an ominous shade of black. Then thunder began to rumble amid the clouds. But as the drinks were served on the covered patio, where it was coolest and where everyone could meet and mingle before the food was served, nobody really bothered too much when, quite suddenly, the storm started and it began pouring with rain.

It was not long afterwards that one of Peter Williamson's children noticed the family's dog, named Scruff, cowering and shivering under a bush on the opposite side of the lawn. Peter immediately resolved to run over and rescue the frightened animal, and told the child to wait where she was until he returned with him. He then dashed across the lawn to retrieve Scruff, but before he got halfway over there was a huge flash of lightning, which zigzagged down across the sky to strike the tree in a neighbour's garden, and as Peter was illuminated by it, with almost every eye watching him from the patio, he vanished from sight, silently and completely. His wife Mary and the children screamed, and the others gasped in absolute astonishment. Then they all ran desperately out into the rain to see what on earth had happened to him. But despite their frantic search, which took them all over the high-walled garden, they found no sign of Peter Williamson anywhere. The man had, or so it seemed, supernaturally disappeared.

Next the police were called, but they had no success in finding the missing Peter either. The only exit from the garden, a door in the wall, was locked (Peter's wife had the key); the wall was too high to climb without a ladder or similar aid; and there were no footprints or other indentations in the flower-beds beneath the wall to suggest that Peter had climbed it. However, the police assumed that he must somehow have absented himself from the garden, yet were at a loss to know how he had actually done it. In fact it was a complete mystery to everyone.

Two days of deep anxiety and much speculation went by. Then without warning, in the early morning of the third day, the Williamsons' gardener found his missing employer lying semi-conscious in some shrubbery at the end of the garden. One of his feet was dangling in a small pool, yet otherwise he was completely dry. The returned Peter Williamson was apparently unharmed, yet he was dressed somewhat differently from when he had vanished. He was straight away taken to the general hospital, accompanied by his relieved and delighted wife, where it was soon determined that apart from being in a state of shock, he was suffering from nothing worse than amnesia. Frustratingly for all concerned, Peter could remember nothing of what had happened to him.

Peter Williamson remained in hospital for one week, then went home to fully recuperate. Yet while he was back, his memory remained tantalizingly blank, although clues to his whereabouts during those sixty lost hours were revealed in a series of disjointed graphic dreams that he soon began having. In them he found himself coming to in another garden, his clothes soaked through, but without knowing where he was or how he had got there. Close by the garden, Peter noticed, there was a narrow road, and he staggered to his feet in the dreams and made for it, then walked along for some distance, until he began to feel so weak and ill that he was obliged to sit down at the side of it to rest.

Fortunately, his dishevelled, wet and pale appearance prompted a passing motorist, who happened to be a doctor, to stop and render assistance, and when he learned that Peter had lost his memory, he kindly drove him to a hospital. There Peter was admitted, but he was completely unable to tell the staff his name or address, and as he carried no identification nothing about him could be thereby ascertained. Yet in the dreams Peter remembered that the ward in which he was placed, which on his arrival seemed to shimmer unnervingly, was named Pritchard, the doctor's name was Nugent, and the ward sister's name was Alice Charles. He also recalled that his voice was slurred and unusually slow, compared with the brisk, clear tones of the doctor and nurses.

Peter dreamed that on the second day at the hospital, when he felt a good deal better, he told the nurse in charge that, as he wanted to get up and take a short walk, he would like to have his clothes. He had been wearing, he knew, a white T-shirt and a pair of blue jeans, as well as his underwear, socks and shoes, but whereas the first and the last three, dried and none the worse for wear, were brought to him, the jeans, he was told, had been too stained and torn to be worth keeping, and had been burned. Help, however, was at hand, as a man in the next bed, noting their similar build, offered to loan Peter a pair of brown corduroy trousers. He gratefully accepted them, slipped on his own clothes and the cords, which were a good fit, and found his legs by exploring the hospital grounds and drinking some tea in its café. He dreamed that he took a longer walk the next day, the third, when he left the hospital, found the road along which he had been brought to get to it, and excitedly followed it until he reached the garden where the dream sequences started. The dreams, he noticed, never went beyond this point.

So clear were the dreams that Peter soon began wondering if they were a recapitulation of what had actually happened to him. His suspicions in this regard were seemingly confirmed when, to his surprise, he came across the brown corduroy trousers, which had been loaned to him by his fellow 'dream' patient, hanging in his wardrobe, where they had been placed by his wife. He knew then that if he could trace the owner, he would be able to both return them and find out where the strange hospital was located. He could see that the cords were new, and from the label inside he found that they had been made by Herbert Cox, a West Country manufacturer; they also bore the owner's initials – J.B. – monogrammed on to the label. Yet when he tried to locate the manufacturer, he discovered to his astonishment that they had closed down in 1954.

Sometime later Peter went to the general hospital for a check-up, and quite by chance he overheard a 'Dr Nugent' being mentioned. He immediately asked where he might find that physician, and was told that Dr Nugent was employed at the cottage hospital that stood, it turned out, not more than half a mile from his own home. Peter barely knew of this hospital's existence, never having been there, as far as he knew, yet it seemed obvious that it must be where the helpful doctor/motorist had taken him. On leaving the general he went straight there, recognizing both the approach road and the hospital and its grounds, and at the reception desk he asked to speak to Dr Nugent, glad that this part of the mystery was apparently about to be solved.

He did not have to wait long for the doctor to make an appearance, and he sprang to his feet as the owner of that familiar face, with its firm jaw and greying temples, walked into the reception area. But Dr Nugent did not return his welcoming smile with the burst of recognition that he had expected; in fact the man did not seem to recognize him at all. So Peter Williamson introduced himself and explained, as Dr Nugent must surely know only too well, that he had been an amnesia victim and was a recent patient of his. The physician looked hard at him, shook his head, then to Peter's absolute incredulity said:

'I'm afraid you have the wrong hospital, old chap. I've never seen you before, and I haven't had an amnesia case for five years.'

Scarcely believing what he heard, Peter protested that the doctor must remember him, but Nugent was adamant that Peter had never been his patient. He could only suggest, by way of explanation, that Peter had heard his name and had seen him, along with Nurse Alice Charles, while they were on a ward round at the general hospital, where they both did occasional work, and that Peter had created a dream scenario involving himself and them both, which he was confusing with reality. This type of dream fantasy, he said, was typical of amnesics. However, he could not explain why Peter was familiar with the cottage hospital's exterior and interior, unless he had actually been there before and had forgotten about it. But the unfaded and brand-new brown corduroy trousers, opined the doctor, must have been loaned to him by a patient at the General Hospital, despite the fact that they had not been on sale anywhere for about twenty years!

At first reading this is a very puzzling case and it is difficult to tell what is going on. After all, if we assume that Peter Williamson did not supernaturally disappear in front of his family and friends, we must explain how he managed to remove himself so quickly from his garden and ask from where he obtained a new pair of corduroy trousers that were no longer sold or manufactured. And if he was not a patient at the cottage hospital, we also need to determine where he spent the three nights and two days that he was missing. He certainly did not pass them lying unconscious in his own garden, for it had been searched both by Mary Williamson and her guests and by the police, but without result – and anyway, how could he have obtained the corduroy trousers if he had been? Peter had suffered a loss of memory, but why? Could the shock of a lightning flash descending nearby cause this, and if so, would it also result in such rapidly-initiated abnormal behaviour?

But the outcome of the alternative possibility – that Peter Williamson did supernaturally disappear – is bizarre, to say the least, although it does perhaps reveal where some go who vanish in such a way. For the spine-chilling answer to Peter's missing days is that he temporarily left our world, in the flash of an eye, and entered another dimension containing its exact duplicate. In that world, incredible though it sounds, life goes on just as it does here, with everything replicated – there's another you and me and Dr Nugent and Nurse Alice Charles – yet although it is generally, it cannot be exactly, synchronized, as the corduroy trousers' manufacturer that went out of business here in 1954 still seemed to be operational in that world's 1974! And although Peter manifested in that world, his counterpart did not immediately vanish from it into this. Hence for a short period there may have been two Peter Williamsons existing in the other dimension, which is why it is just as well that he lost his memory or otherwise he might have gone to 'his' home there and bumped into 'himself'! One wonders who would have been more shocked!

Finally, we must take note of the similar weather conditions accompanying three of these disappearances. Both Nancy Camel, it is said, and Peter Williamson vanished during a thunderstorm, while one erupted soon after the disappearance of Owen Parfitt. I have already pointed out that thunderstorms were part of the scenario of some ancient supernatural disappearances. This suggests that either the thunderstorms themselves or the atmospheric conditions leading up to them may somehow be responsible, in part if not wholly, for the instantaneous disappearance of a human body from this world and its subsequent reappearance in another dimension of being.

If so, then it explains why Zeus, the Greek god of thunder and lightning, was said to have snatched away Ganymedes and Ixion, and to have ordered the similar removal from earth of Alcmene.

7   Benjamin Bathurst's Trousers

He stayd not for more bidding, but away
Was suddein vanished out of his sight ...
They lookt about, but nowhere could espye
Tract of his foot: then dead through great affright
They both nigh were, and each bad other flye:
Both fled attonce, ne ever backe retourned eye.

From *The Faerie Queene*, book II, canto III, by Edmund
Spenser

Although the sudden and enigmatic departure of Owen Parfitt from the world, as detailed in the last chapter, suggests that he vanished supernaturally, we cannot of course be absolutely certain that this was the case. All we know is that during the space of about fifteen minutes a crippled old man disappeared from outside the front door of his cottage and was neither seen nor heard of again. In this respect his disappearance is as much of a mystery today as it was in 1768.

There are a number of these 'borderline' cases, and none is perhaps more famous than the strange disappearance of His Majesty's Special Envoy Benjamin Bathurst at Perleberg in 1809. His unexplained loss caused a sensation at the time and it has been the subject of much speculation ever since. I shall therefore consider it in some detail and try to take a fresh walk along some familiar pathways.

At about noon on Saturday 25 November 1809, a post-chaise pulled up outside the post-house of the small and unattractive German town of Perleberg, which stands beside the River Stepnitz

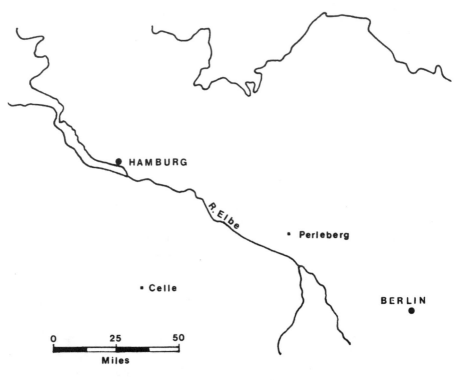

Figure 3   Map showing the position of Perleberg

midway between Berlin and Hamburg (see Figure 3).

Within the post-chaise were three men, one of whom was the young, handsome Benjamin Bathurst, dashingly and expensively clad in a cloak made of sable fur with a violet-coloured velvet lining, a grey travelling suit with a frog-band holding two pistols, and a fur hat. A diamond clip secured the scarf in place around his neck. His anxious look and trembling fingers revealed that he was in the grip of some strange terror. His companions, who were also tense but less obviously nervous, were a German-born embassy messenger named Krouse (or Krause), and Bathurst's valet Nikolaus Hilbert, who was Swiss.

The three descended quickly from the coach and entered the post-house, where fresh horses were requested, for they were keen to continue their journey to the next town of Leutzen as soon as possible. Yet during the comparatively short waiting time while this was being done, Benjamin Bathurst, who was travelling under the pseudonym of Koch and posing as a businessman, had a fatal change of mind. He evidently decided that instead of going on by daylight, it would be safer if they waited until nightfall. He therefore countermanded his order for the horses and made some enquiries about eating establishments in Perleberg. Then he left the post-house with his companions and together they walked, following the directions given, about one hundred yards along the main street to the White Swan inn, which stood close by the Parchimer gate, through which the road continued to Hamburg. There they ordered a meal.

The reason why Benjamin Bathurst was travelling incognito and why he was extremely agitated, and why indeed he decided to delay his journey until nightfall, was because he considered himself to be in grave danger of being stopped and arrested, perhaps even murdered, by French troops, who were then busy clearing the area, at the invitation of the Prussian government, of vagabonds, footpads, and other criminals and undesirables. The 25-year-old Bathurst felt threatened in this way because he was returning from a secret diplomatic mission in Vienna, where he had been instrumental in persuading the Austrians to take up arms against the French, with the object of thereby relieving the British troops fighting against Napoleon in Spain. But the Austrians had been defeated by an angry Napoleon, who hurriedly marched his armies to crush them, and were forced to sign a humiliating peace treaty, which resulted in Bathurst's desperate ride across Europe, dodging the enemy whom he felt sure was searching for him, heading for Hamburg where he hoped to take a boat to England.

Such was Benjamin Bathurst's fear of arrest or assassination, that having eaten dinner at the White Swan, he then made his way to the nearby Prussian army post, where he told the commander, Captain Klitzing, that he believed his life to be in danger and asked for an armed guard. This was quickly granted, despite Klitzing's evident belief that the anxieties of the young 'businessman' were groundless. However, Captain Klitzing could not help but notice 'Herr Koch's' pale face and shaking hands, nor the difficulty he had in putting back on his exquisite sable cloak. This is perhaps why he detailed two cuirassiers to return with the frightened man to the White Swan and to position themselves outside the front door. He may also have suspected that 'Herr Koch' was a far more important person than he claimed to be.

Thus guarded, Benjamin Bathurst retired to a room in the White Swan, where he read through the diplomatic papers he carried with him, apparently burned several of them, and wrote some letters. Later, he was observed in another room, possibly the kitchen, injudiciously playing with his valuable watch and taking out a bag full of money, watched by various members of staff, one of whom was a servant named Christian Mertens (of whom more later). These diversions occupied Benjamin Bathurst until about seven o'clock in the evening, when he suddenly and unaccountably dismissed the cuirassiers loaned him by Captain Klitzing and ordered the post-chaise with its fresh horses to be brought outside the inn at nine o'clock, when he intended to set off again with his two companions, Krouse and Hilbert.

At that time the post-house in Perleberg was run by the Schmidt family, which consisted of its head, the elderly ostler Herr Schmidt, his wife Frau Schmidt, their no-good son August, reputedly a gambler and a wastrel, and a younger daughter, all of whom were assisted in their various tasks, which included the delivery of letters, by the Schmidts' servant girl Elizabeth Nagel.

When the Schmidts had changed the horses of the post-chaise, the equipage was walked along Perleberg's main street to the White Swan inn by Frau Schmidt, who lit her way by holding aloft a horn lantern. Once the horses had been brought to a halt outside the inn, a further period of waiting began, during which time Frau Schmidt gave charge of the horses to her son August and her daughter, who soon tired of waiting and handed them over to the dutiful Elizabeth Nagel.

But finally the travellers were ready to depart. The diplomatic trunk belonging to Benjamin Bathurst was first placed on top of the post-chaise, watched from the steps by its owner, who was eager to be off again. The landlord of the White Swan stood in the doorway taking payment for the meals and rented room from messenger Krouse; Benjamin Bathurst's valet Hilbert waited by the coach door for his master to enter; and Elizabeth Nagel assisted the postilion in making some last minute adjustments to the horses' harnesses.

It was in the next few moments that Benjamin Bathurst, His

Majesty's Special Envoy, mysteriously disappeared. In the unpublished diary of George Cotsford Call, Benjamin Bathurst's brother-in-law, who accompanied his sister to Perleberg in June 1810, seeking information about the disappearance, he describes it thus:

> The horses were ordered out of the carriage [?] at the door of the inn of a town walled like Launceston; Mr Bathurst went aside from the carriage, and was never seen afterwards. The messenger waited, expecting his return every moment, and when it was found that he came not the authorities interfered ... No clue could be found to account for Mr B's disappearance, though the country was scoured in all directions.

Likewise, the account of Bathurst's vanishing printed in a German serial publication devoted to crime and criminal cases called *Neue Pitaval*, or New Pitaval, the first edition of which appeared in 1842, briefly relates that 'during the time of packing the carriage ... one of the travellers [i.e. Bathurst] absented himself, and returned no more. Waiting for him, looking for him, calling him – all were in vain. Up to this day he has never returned.'

By contrast, the writer Sabine Baring-Gould, in his article entitled 'The Disappearance of Bathurst' published in the *Cornhill Magazine* of March 1887, rather more graphically claims that

> he [Bathurst] stood outside the inn watching his portmanteau, which had been taken within, being replaced on the carriage, stepped round to the heads of the horses – and was never seen again. It must be remembered that this was the end of November. Darkness had closed in before 5 p.m., as the sun set at four. An oil lantern hung across the street, emitting a feeble light; the ostler had a horn lantern. No one particularly observed the movements of Mr Bathurst at the moment. He had gone to the horses' heads, where the ostler's lantern had fallen on him ... Suddenly, inexplicably, without a word, a cry, an alarm of any sort, he was gone – spirited away, and what really became of him will never be known with certainty.

It took several minutes for an alarm to be raised. When it was realized that Benjamin Bathurst was no longer in the street, the interior of the inn was first checked to make sure that he had not re-entered it unobserved, and when that search failed to locate him, he was called out for but without response. Puzzlement quickly became anxiety. Then Krouse went to enquire if by chance his master had called on Captain Klitzing again. This too proved negative, although Klitzing, recalling Bathurst's nervousness and sensing that the young man's fears had perhaps become a horrible reality, took immediate steps to try and find him. He ordered his men to seize the post-chaise and the belongings of Bathurst, placed a guard around the White Swan inn, and had Krouse and Hilbert driven to another inn, where they were lodged under guard. The following morning, with Bathurst still missing, he organized a thorough search of the town and the surrounding countryside, which went on for several days and which included dragging the Stepnitz river. Bloodhounds were also employed. But no trace of Benjamin Bathurst was found.

It was soon determined, however, that two fur cloaks, one owned by Krouse, the other, the sable fur with the violet-coloured velvet lining, belonging to Bathurst, were missing. A search for them was at once initiated. This of course means that Bathurst was not wearing his fur cloak while waiting to board the post-chaise, which is odd because the night was very cold. The explanation for this may be that both it and Krouse's cloak were stolen somewhat earlier in the evening, which would account for the party's delay in setting off. It may also be the reason why Bathurst, as reported by Baring-Gould, stepped round to the head of the horses, for these were then being held by Elizabeth Nagel, the servant girl of the Schmidt family, and he doubtless wished to ask her if she knew anything about the missing furs.

If Benjamin Bathurst had suspicions about the honesty of the Schmidts he had good reason, because a few days later the authorities rigorously interrogated Nagel, who broke down and told them that Frau Schmidt had both furs in her possession. The Schmidts' home was searched and the furs were found, Benjamin Bathurst's having been placed in a sack and hidden under a pile of firewood by August Schmidt. The discovery led to the arrest and incarceration of the entire Schmidt family, who were naturally

suspected of being responsible for Benjamin Bathurst's disappearance. Yet all denied knowing anything about it or of having
anything to do with it, Frau Schmidt claiming that the furs had
been stolen by her at the post-house, where they had been left by
the travellers. But this must be untrue, at least in part, because
although Krouse may have left his fur there, Benjamin Bathurst
certainly did not, as he was wearing his when he left the White
Swan inn to visit Captain Klitzing. As far as is known, he did not
return to the post-house at any time, which naturally suggests that
someone at the White Swan stole it later on and subsequently
passed it to Frau Schmidt, who acted therefore as a receiver.

The next major development happened exactly three weeks
later on Saturday 16 December, when two peasant women, who
were out collecting firewood in a copse about two miles from
Perleberg, found a pair of men's trousers lying stretched out on the
grass. They were turned inside out and sodden with water from the
recent rains, and they were punctured by two bullet holes,
although there was no sign of any bloodstains on the fabric.
Turning the trousers (which have also been described as
'pantaloons' and 'overalls') right side out, the women noticed
earth marks on the outside and found a short, yet unfinished letter
written in pencil in one of the pockets. They immediately carried
the trousers into Perleberg and handed them over to the
authorities, whose investigations revealed that they belonged to
Benjamin Bathurst, and that the letter they contained was in his
handwriting and was directed to his wife, Phillida.

The trousers – which were not the grey ones worn by Benjamin
Bathurst on his arrival at Perleberg – were the last clue to be
discovered, yet they were more of an enigma than a clue. It was
soon realized, for example, that they could not have lain in the
wood for more than a few hours, as otherwise the notepaper on
which the letter was written would have disintegrated in the heavy
rain that had fallen in the previous week. The wood had also been
searched some days before without them being seen, although
they surely would have been noticed if they had been there then.
Who therefore had placed them there, and why? They bore two
bullet holes, yet the lack of bloodstains and the exact alignment of
the holes indicated that they were not being worn when the shots
were fired into them. What then did the gunman, whoever he was,

hope to achieve by such a strange act?

But perhaps the real clue lies in the letter. I have not been able to trace a copy of the original, but this is what Benjamin Bathurst's sister, Mrs Tryphena Thistlethwayte, says about its contents in her book *Memoirs and Correspondence of Henry Bathurst, Lord Bishop of Norwich*:

> It contained a representation of the dangers to which he was exposed, in consequence of his being surrounded by enemies, and expressed great fears that he should never reach England; and that his ruin would be brought about by Count D'Entraigues and the Russians. It contained also a request to her not to marry again, in the event of his not returning. These, with a few words on other subjects, were scrawled in pencil, and were sent with the overalls to his wife, and were the last trace of him ever discovered.

Benjamin Bathurst dearly loved his wife Phillida, who was ten years his senior and by whom he had had three children, two girls – Rosa and Emma – and an infant son, who was evidently born after he left England for Vienna and whom he never saw. It therefore seems entirely out of character for him to have 'scrawled in pencil' what he thought might have been his last letter to his wife. He had been supplied with pen and ink at the White Swan, and he would surely have written a letter with these in a fair hand to her. Moreover, if he really thought that death might come at any moment on the road out of Perleberg, he would certainly also have posted the letter before he left that wretched little German town. He knew where the post-house was; he had a servant to take it there for him; and he knew that, if he preferred, he could give it directly to one or other of the Schmidts when the post-chaise was brought to the door of the White Swan inn.

But let us suppose for a moment that Bathurst had been knocked unconscious by an assailant (or assailants) in the road outside the White Swan inn and had then been carried off into the darkness to a nearby house, where he was robbed of his money and possessions. On regaining consciousness, he would presumably have found himself bound and gagged, a captive. His abductors must have wondered what on earth they should do with him, particularly as they were in fear of discovery by Captain

Klitzing's search party, which forcibly entered and minutely examined many homes in Perleberg. Might they therefore, in order to throw the searchers off the scent, have forced Bathurst to write a letter to his wife in which he expressed a belief that his life was in danger from a Frenchman, the Count D'Entraigues, and from the Russians, all foreigners like himself? Because they wanted the letter to be read, and noting the inclemency of the weather, they therefore made him write it in pencil, as this would not be washed away in the rain like ink. Letter-writing in such a situation would naturally account for Bathurst's hurried scrawl. His captors of course forgot that paper soon turns into a pulpy mush in rain water, although they were incredibly lucky in this regard, for the letter was found before that happened. We may suppose that Bathurst, his hands free, made a desperate attempt to escape before he finished writing it, and was either deliberately or accidentally killed, the letter being afterwards placed in his trouser pocket, and the trousers pulled off him, thereby turning them inside out. The pair of red herrings were eventually taken to the wood, where perhaps two shots were fired into them by the panicky and none too bright murderers, and left for someone to find.

But whose house might have been used for the concealment of the abducted Benjamin Bathurst? It must have stood close by the White Swan inn but it could not have been owned or inhabited by known criminals or suspicious characters, such as the Schmidt family, as otherwise it would have been at or near the top of a search list. Yet if a previously blameless servant like Christian Mertens was involved in the crime, who worked at the White Swan inn and who had seen the wealth that Benjamin Bathurst had ostentatiously displayed, then his house, standing on the other side of the Parchimer Gate, would be both conveniently placed and unlikely to be entered by a search party.

Hence it is possible that moments before Benjamin Bathurst was about to board the post-chaise, he walked around to Elizabeth Nagel who was holding the horses in order to ask her if she knew anything about the disappearance of his fur cloak, and was clubbed unconscious by either Christian Mertens or Augustus Schmidt, caught before he collapsed on the ground, and quickly carried off down the dark street to Mertens's house. This assault would only have taken a few moments and none of those waiting upon Benjamin Bathurst would have known what had happened. As far as they were concerned he inexplicably vanished.

Such a scenario is made initially more plausible if I now reveal that in April 1852, a skeleton was discovered either underneath the kitchen floor (according to Mrs Thistlethwayte) or under the stone threshold of the stable (according to Baring-Gould) at the Mertens' house (then lived in by another family, Christian Mertens having died in 1834). The find, made forty-three years after Bathurst's disappearance, forms a strange parallel with the skeleton unearthed in a garden in Shepton Mallet forty-five years after the vanishing of Owen Parfitt. The Perleberg skeleton, however, was male and the skull was distinguished by its fine set of teeth – and Benjamin Bathurst had had a fine set of teeth! More ominously, the skull had been fractured at the back by the man having been struck with an axe or similar implement. There was no sign of any clothing with the skeleton, which suggests that the victim had been stripped before being interred.

It has also been thought incriminating that Christian Mertens, who did little more than shine boots and perform other odd jobs at the White Swan inn, was able, upon the marriages of his two daughters, to give one £150 and the other £120. These are very large sums of money for a servant to have accumulated in the early years of the nineteenth century and seemingly point to Mertens having obtained them dishonestly, by for example robbing Benjamin Bathurst, the wealthy Englishman, who stayed briefly at his place of employment.

But the evidence against Mertens is largely circumstantial. For a start, he was known in Perleberg, according to Sabine Baring-Gould, as an industrious, honest and respectable family man, who saved rather than spent money. However, against this rather rosy image of Mertens must be set Tryphena Thistleth-wayte's remark that 'the porter was said to have been a man of bad character'.

But if we can believe Baring-Gould, Mertens was the type of man who, though low-paid, could have endowed his daughters with the sums of money mentioned, especially if he had started saving for their marriages when they were born. After all, to accumulate £270 in, say, twenty years would only have required him to put aside £13.50 a year, less if interest was earned on the capital, or 26 pence (about five English shillings) a week. He might conceivably have earned this amount in tips at the White Swan inn.

The presence of the skeleton beneath the kitchen floor is only damaging to him if it was positively identified as being that of Benjamin Bathurst or, if not, it was shown to have been placed there sometime during his occupancy of the building (1803–1834). But neither was proved to be the case. The date of a person's burial is very difficult to establish once the flesh has rotted away without making use of chemical tests that were unavailable in 1852. Hence the murder and the victim's burial could have preceded Merten's occupany of the house or succeeded it; or they may have taken place while he lived there. We simply don't know.

It was assumed at the time of its discovery that the skeleton belonged to Benjamin Bathurst, but a positive identification was never made. In fact the opposite was concluded by Mrs Thistlethwayte, who visited Perleberg's chief magistrate to find out more about it and was shown the skeleton's skull by him. This is what she said about the incident:

He then produced part of the under-jaw, which had very fine teeth, and only one double tooth missing: the right side of the jaw was broken off. I could not, of course, identify this relic; I could only say I remembered that my poor brother had remarkably fine teeth; but many persons have the same. On showing the miniature portrait [of Benjamin Bathurst] to the chief magistrate, he said that, as a medical man, he could attest that the jaw did not belong to the person whose portrait I produced. He then exhibited the skull. The moment I saw this, I could decidedly pronounce it was not my poor brother's ... The part of the skull which was shown to me was very low in the forehead, and rather prominent, with great indenture between that and the nose, and the whole very short; all of which was exactly the opposite to my brother's head; he having a high forehead, and straight to the tip of his nose in profile – the Grecian form. I had therefore no hesitation in making this confident declaration.

It may be objected that Mrs Thistlethwayte had not seen her

brother for forty-three years and was thus hardly qualified to judge whether the skull belonged to him or not, particularly as skulls are notoriously difficult to identify. Yet the two features she particularly noted, the low forehead and the deficient nose bridge, were so unlike those of her brother that she may well have been entirely correct in her conclusions, which gain strength from the chief magistrate's opinion of the jaw. If so, we are left with the question: what happened to Benjamin Bathurst?

Various explanations were made at the time and have been since. These include a) he slipped away and, by reason of insanity, committed suicide; b) he left Perleberg and went alone to the coast, only to be drowned while crossing over to Sweden by boat; and c) he was captured (when attempting to leave Perleberg alone) by mounted French customs officers and taken by them to the fortress at Magdeburg, where he was imprisoned and later murdered.

Astrologically minded readers will appreciate that as Benjamin Bathurst, born on 14 March 1784, was a Pisces native he belonged to the most unstable and psychologically vulnerable zodiac group. He was certainly in a highly agitated state when he arrived at Perleberg, and while there he behaved both precipitously and irrationally. He had experienced some form of mental breakdown in the previous year and he may even have been a little deranged. Yet there is absolutely no reason to think that he took his own life, especially as his body would certainly have been found if he had.

Nor is there any reason for thinking that he deserted his companions as they were all about to leave Perleberg, vanished into the darkness of the night, and left the town on foot. He must have known that he would have been far more at risk of being captured and murdered, by common criminals or by the French, had he done so.

This means that Benjamin Bathurst was either assaulted and carried off outside the White Swan inn, or that he supernaturally disappeared. Let us examine each possibility more closely.

A successful assault would have required the planned cooperation of two men and sufficient darkness and/or lack of witnesses to make their attack undetectable. But given the seeming impossibility of two such men finding the opportunity of making away with Benjamin Bathurst without being seen, it is hardly creditable that they would have even considered trying to do it, however much they might have wished to. They could not have known or even suspected that Bathurst would walk around to the 'heads of the horses', if indeed he did, so why should they hide themselves nearby in case he did? And had they just happened to be loitering nearby when Bathurst came up and took the opportunity of knocking him out, then their presence would almost certainly have been noticed by one or other of the people at or near the White Swan front door.

Sabine Baring-Gould has made much of the darkness of Perleberg's main street and has also portrayed it as being completely devoid of human life, with the exception of those waiting upon Benjamin Bathurst. But in both these respects he is demonstrably quite wrong. The street may have lacked the equivalent of modern street lighting, but it did receive some illumination from the windows of the houses flanking it and from the oil lamps suspended across it (one of which he mentions). But he has forgotten to take into account the most important source of light – the moon. I have calculated that there was a full moon on 22 November 1809, which means there was a waning but otherwise very large lunar disc in the sky on the evening of 25 November. The moonlight falling on Perleberg might have been lessened by cloud cover, but if the temperature was as cold as the wearing of fur cloaks suggests, then the sky must have been clear. The streets of Perleberg, particularly its widest thoroughfare, the main street, would therefore have been quite brightly lit, notwithstanding the dark shadows that the moonlight would have thrown across or alongside some of them.

Furthermore, Perleberg's main street would normally have been quite busy at 9 p.m. on a Saturday night, when people were out relaxing after a hard week's work. Some of them might have been taking a walk, while others would have been going into or coming out of the town's hotels and hostelries, like the White Swan. But on Saturday 25 November, the main street would have been particularly busy, as there was a big social event, namely a ball for the local nobility, taking place that evening at the Crown Hotel. This establishment stood, like the post-house, at the opposite end of the street, which meant that all traffic going to it, whether on foot, horseback, or riding in carriages, coming from the west, must have entered the town (which was, as George Call observed, 'walled like Launceston') via the Parchimer Gate and proceeded there past the White Swan.

The combination of relatively good visibility and numerous passers-by make it highly unlikely, if not impossible, that Benjamin Bathurst could have been knocked unconscious outside the White Swan inn and afterwards carried off without his assailants being observed by someone. Neither could he have been killed in the street by a blow from an axe delivered to the back of his head, as this would have spilled a lot of incriminating blood on to the cobblestones, and none was found. We must also remember that a blow to the head struck with either a blunt instrument or an axe makes a singular and audible sound, that Benjamin Bathurst would have collapsed immediately to the ground, falling too quickly to be caught, thereby making another singular and audible sound, and that the horses would certainly have started in fright. Yet nothing unusual was heard or seen by those nearby.

The suddenness, silence and completeness of Benjamin Bathurst's disappearance, happening as it did within a few feet of other people (considerably less where Elizabeth Nagel was concerned), suggests that he vanished supernaturally. This is why it is important to remember that fright, such as that which gripped Bathurst throughout his stay at Perleberg, is one of the apparent precursors of the supernatural disappearance. The supernatural disappearance can therefore be a protective mechanism, which can happen to certain individuals in moments of crisis, notably when they are facing death. If so, Benjamin Bathurst's increasing fear as he left the relative security of the White Swan inn to be driven into the hostile countryside (as he perceived it) outside Perleberg presumably acted as the switch to remove him from the scene.

But what of the trousers belonging to him that were discovered three weeks later in a copse? Surely their existence reveals that His Majesty's Special Envoy did not vanish into thin air?

The trousers are admittedly a problem, although they may point to the opposite conclusion. In fact they may show that Benjamin Bathurst not only supernaturally disappeared but was transported into another dimension.

What is particularly significant about the trousers is that they appeared in the copse only hours before they were found by the two peasant women. Had they been placed there the day before, or if the women had postponed their visit until the following day, the letter they contained would have turned to pulp. With such strangely exact timing, it seems that someone or something knew that the women would go to the copse that day.

We have no idea if the peasant women planned their outing, but if they did it seems highly unlikely that their plans could have reached the ears of Benjamin Bathurst's murderer or murderers, if he or they existed. Hence was it an entirely lucky accident that the trousers were placed in the copse on that day – or might they have been directed there then by some outside power or entity which knew of the peasant women's intentions and made use of them? It is perhaps helpful to remember that a mysterious pair of trousers formed part of the Peter Williamson disappearance. When he vanished, Williamson apparently rematerialized in another dimension, one similar in every way to our own, where his own jeans were removed and destroyed, and where he was loaned a new pair of corduroy trousers. The latter came with him when he was returned to our world. If true, it shows that people and objects can move in both directions across the divide which separates here from there and retain their integrity.

Let us suppose therefore that upon supernaturally disappearing in Perleberg Benjamin Bathurst slipped immediately into that other dimension. We would not expect him to have materialized in the other Perleberg's main street, but he may have done so in the countryside near to the town. He would not of course have known he was in another dimension when he regained consciousness (if he indeed lost it), and on looking about him he would certainly have been very confused; he may even have feared that he had been abducted. If so, surely only that clever French spy Count D'Entraigues could have whisked him away from under the noses of his companions! Or the treacherous Russians!

But once Bathurst discovered that he was unhurt, unbound and alone he would have taken immediate advantage of his freedom and moved off, perhaps to eventually take shelter in the simulacrum of the little copse where his trousers were found. There he would have stayed until morning, shivering and unhappy, totally unable to account for the situation he found himself in, and thinking only of his beloved wife and children.

When the sun rose, and finding a scrap of paper and a pencil in one of his pockets, he perhaps passed half an hour writing to Phillida, his cold fingers and the fact that his knee was his desk accounting for his scrawled handwriting. The writing was psychologically comforting, diverting his attention from his miserable predicament and allowing him to express his darkest fears. Then it suddenly began raining. He cursed, and thrust the unfinished letter into a pocket of his trousers. He pressed himself against the trunk of one of the leafless trees, trying to keep dry while deciding what his next move should be.

When the rain finally stopped and the sun came out, Benjamin Bathurst immediately began removing his outer garments, whose wetness was threatening to soak through his other clothes to his skin. His clinging outer trousers or overalls turned themselves inside out as he pushed them down past his knees. He had just yanked them off over his feet and laid them on the ground, when he caught sight of two figures walking towards the copse across the fields. They were some distance away but he could see that they were armed with rifles. Terror clutched at his throat until he thought he would choke. They were coming for him! Without thinking, he turned and fled, away from the copse and his pursuers. God give me the strength, he prayed as he ran, to get to the coast, to get back to England, to feel again the loving arms of my darling Phillida!

But the approaching men, as it happened, were neither French nor were they looking for him. They were two country youths out hunting for rabbits, which is why each carried a musket primed with powder and ball. They dearly wanted to shoot a rabbit, for the fun as much as for the feast it would provide, but the little blighters were keeping their furry heads down that morning. They had had no luck at all. The youths decided to walk as far as the copse, and then return home.

They got a surprise when they reached it. Someone had left his trousers on the ground! They nudged one another and laughed coarsely. 'He got lucky, but we didn't!' snarled one, expressing his sexual jealousy and his frustration with their wasted outing. Then he lifted his musket impulsively to his shoulder and fired at the trousers. 'Take that, you dirty bastard!' he cried. His friend yelped appreciatively and not to be outdone, discharged his musket into the same leg of the pants. Then they both turned to one another and laughed loudly again. At least they had shot something!

But their guffaws came to an abrupt halt when they looked back at the trousers – or at least back at where they had been. For there was now no sign of them. The patch of stunted grass was completely bare. The youths stared at the spot, trying to understand what had happened, their mouths dropping open to reveal their rotten teeth. Then they cried out like wounded animals and fled in terror.

But we know what happened to Benjamin Bathurst's vanishing trousers. They recrossed the divide between the two worlds, wafted into this dimension either by the power of Benjamin Bathurst's love for his wife or perhaps by some unknown but clearly romantic intelligence, and settled in the same spot here on 16 December 1809, where they were found by two peasant women out collecting sticks.

I cannot tell you if Benjamin Bathurst's trousers were held between the two dimensions for those three weeks or if time there passes much more slowly than it does here, like it does in the world of the fairies.

But then, some things have to remain a secret, don't they?

Phillida Bathurst never did marry again, even though she lived until her eighties. And her husband's loss was not the only tragedy the poor woman had to bear, as two curious accidents, both of which took place at Rome, deprived her of two of her children. Her son was killed when he fell from his mount while taking part in a horse race, and her eldest daughter Rosa, who was celebrated for her beauty, was, on 24 March 1824, thrown from her horse into the River Tiber, wherein she drowned.

8   Going, Going, Gone

Norna returned no answer whatever to his repeated invocations and the company began to look upon each other with some surprise, when the Udaller, raising the skin which covered the entrance of the tent, discovered that the interior was empty. The wonder was now general, and not unmixed with fear; for it seemed impossible that Norna could have, in any manner, escaped from the tabernacle in which she was enclosed without having been discovered by the company. Gone, however, she was, and the Udaller, after a moment's consideration, dropt the skin-curtain again over the entrance of the tent.

From *The Pirate* by Sir Walter Scott

Another remarkable disappearance took place in Germany only four years after Benjamin Bathurst vanished. The case is made even stranger by the fact that it involved two people, who although unrelated, looked so alike as to be mistaken for twin brothers.

In 1810, at Aguila, an officer of Napoleon's Imperial Army, Captain Alswanger, met a man who was literally his double. This happened when Alswanger and a group of fellow officers entered a café for some refreshment, and were astonished to see a man seated within who could have been the captain's twin brother. In fact the tall, good-looking Captain Alswanger was so amazed by their remarkable similarity that he offered to make the fellow, whose name was Diderici, his valet. Diderici, who was then earning a precarious living by busking with his guitar, jumped at the chance of improving his lot in life, and was further gratified to find that he and his new master quickly became friends. Captain Alswanger soon took advantage of their likeness to play jokes on his comrades and to have Diderici stand in for him at boring army functions. And Diderici – a Salzburg tradesman's son – was able to experience at first-hand the life and social position enjoyed by the captain. Helped by the acting skills he had developed while touring some months earlier with a troupe of players, it wasn't long before Diderici could impersonate Captain Alswanger with exactitude.

All went well until one day, shortly after Alswanger's regiment had been posted to Danzig (modern Gdansk), the handsome and popular captain suffered a stroke and died. He was found stretched out on the floor of his quarters by Diderici, who took the opportunity of literally stepping into his master's shoes. He changed clothes with the corpse, let it be known that Diderici had died, and from that moment on became Captain Alswanger.

This unlikely changeover is not without its precedents. It is known, for example, that the Syrian king, Antiochus II, was impersonated after his death by his double Artemon. Antiochus was poisoned by his wife Laodice, by whom he had two sons, after he had married another woman for political purposes. Laodice then made Artemon take to the king's bed and pretend that he, as king, was ill. The sick 'monarch' lost no time in appointing Seleucus, one of Laodice's sons, his heir to the throne, and upon apparently dying of natural causes, Seleucus was crowned king. He quickly secured his position by ordering the death of the king's second wife and her son.

Diderici fooled everyone, including members of the real Captain Alswanger's family (who lived in Rome), with his impersonation, and he might successfully have taken over his master's life had he not foolishly stolen a gold ring set with a large carbuncle from the man with whom he was then lodging at Danzig. Needing money, he sold the ring to another citizen. But this man, when out one day in the Danzig market, entered quite by chance into conversation with its real owner, who, recognizing his ring and demanding to know from where he had obtained it, quickly summoned the guard. They soon determined that the thief, to everyone's amazement, was Captain Alswanger.

Diderici, alias Captain Alswanger, was brought before the Court of Inquiry, headed by Danzig's Governor-General Rapp, and he soon broke down and confessed to both the theft and to his imposture. The Court was naturally amazed, and Governor-General Rapp very angered, by the deception. Rapp sent word to Napoleon, informing him of Diderici's wrongdoings and asking what punishment he should be given. Napoleon was deeply insulted that a commoner from Salzburg should have fooled his fellow Frenchmen with his impersonation and brought dishonour with his thieving upon the Imperial Army. He ordered him to be branded as a common criminal, placed temporarily in the notorious Weichselmunde fortress, and then later transferred to a prison ship at Brest for life. At Weichselmunde, the newly branded Diderici was put in Cell 80 and subjected to the prison's harsh and degrading regime.

But two years later, in 1813, the French returned the fortress to its builders, the Prussians, and announced that an amnesty had been granted to all French military prisoners, regardless of their crimes. Yet when they began releasing the French Imperial Army prisoners, they discovered that Cell 80 was empty. On enquiring what had happened to its occupant, the prisoner Diderici, they were told by the jailer that he had unaccountably and mysteriously disappeared. This had happened one day when Diderici and the other prisoners were being exercised.

According to one version of the incident, Diderici suddenly and unaccountably began fading from view in front of his startled jail-mates. Then, to their absolute astonishment, he vanished completely from sight and his chains fell with a clank and a rattle on to the ground.

But the jailer, who perhaps realized that such a story would not be believed, contrived to make it more palatable.

'One day,' he said, 'when the prisoners were out in the grounds for exercise. No 80 suddenly disappeared ... it was an extraordinary thing to happen, and all we can think of to account for it is that the prisoner may have jumped into the Vistula, which flows past the fortress, and drowned.'

He omitted to mention that Diderici had neither the freedom of movement nor the opportunity to jump into the Vistula, and that even if by some miracle he had done, he would certainly have been seen by the other prisoners and/or the guards.

Another puzzling early nineteenth-century disappearance, which took place on the Isle of Wight, has a strange connection with a romantic tragedy that happened in the fourteenth century.

Apparently, in the year 1364 a knight named Edward Estur,

who lived in the village of Gatcombe, joined a crusade to the Holy Land, taking with him his beloved mistress Lucy Lightfoot. Wishing to keep Lucy safe from danger Edward settled her in Cyprus, and vowed to return for her when he and his fellow knights had defeated the Saracens in Syria. But unfortunately, while there, Edward received a severe head wound which caused him to develop amnesia. He not only forgot all about his promise to Lucy but he forgot all about her, and he returned home alone to Gatcombe. The lovers never saw each other again, and the abandoned Lucy died of a broken heart. When Edward Estur passed away many years later he was buried in Gatcombe Church, where an effigy was erected to his memory.

Then in 1830, a teenage girl from the nearby village of Bowcombe, whose name was also Lucy Lightfoot or who had adopted that appellation, began visiting Gatcombe Church to admire the effigy of Edward. It wasn't long before she seemed to become infatuated with it, and she would ride over regularly from Bowcombe to spend hours sitting in the church gazing up at his stone face. When asked why she did such a thing, she replied: 'I love him in my thoughts and in my dreams.' Her strange obsession went on for many months and continued until she entered Gatcombe Church on 13 June 1831, when a violent thunderstorm suddenly broke out and, it is rumoured, the sky was darkened by an eclipse. When the storm had passed, the girl's trembling horse was found still tethered to its post, but the girl herself had unaccountably disappeared. She was never heard of or seen again, and her fate is as much a mystery today as it was in 1831.

Just over forty years later, in 1873, another supernatural disappearance, one involving a young married couple, took place at an English hotel. However, neither of the people concerned vanished but instead parts of the room in which they were staying, albeit temporarily. The incident was so bizarre that it was reported by *The Times* of London, although the newspaper's editor felt obliged to negate the couple's account of what had happened to them, by running the story under the title of 'Extraordinary Hallucination'.

On the evening of Monday 8 December 1873, in Bristol, Thomas and Annie Cumpston, who were *en route* from Clifton to Weston-super-Mare, booked into the Victoria Hotel, which stood

near to the town's main railway station, in order to catch the first
train to Weston-super-Mare the following morning. The
Cumpstons, who resided in Virginia Road, Leeds, were by all
accounts a well-off respectable couple, although the 25-year-old
Mr Cumpston did have a speech impediment and also carried, as it
was later revealed, a formidable arsenal of weapons, namely three
knives and a pistol. His possession of the latter may be explained
by the fact that handguns could then be bought over the counter at
gun shops, and because the city streets of Victorian Britain were
hazardous places in which to be.

The Cumpstons went to bed at about midnight, but at one
o'clock they were suddenly disturbed by the sound of loud voices
which apparently came from an adjacent room. They fetched the
landlady, Mrs Tongue, who told them that they must have been
mistaken, as the voices could no longer be heard when she entered
the room. The Cumpstons, somewhat nonplussed, returned to bed
and all remained quiet for about two hours. What happened next
terrified them both. This is the account given by *The Bristol Daily
Post*:

> About three or four o'clock they heard worse noises, but
> what they were they had no idea. The floor seemed to be
> giving way, and the bed also seemed to open. They heard
> voices, and what they said was repeated after them. Her
> husband wished her to get out of the way. The floor certainly
> seemed to open, and her husband fell down some distance,
> and she tried to get him up. She asked him to discharge his
> pistols to frighten anybody who might be near, and he fired
> his revolver into the ceiling. They got out of the window, but
> she did not know how, being so frightened; and when they
> got to the ground she asked him to fire off another shot,
> which he did.

The bed also 'did all sorts of strange things' which were not
specified, and the floor apparently opened or disappeared to
reveal a ghastly blackness, from which the mocking, echo-like
voices came, and into which Thomas Cumpston half-fell and had
to be dragged from by his wife. It may be that Mr Cumpston came
close to inadvertently dropping through the divide which separates
this dimension from the next and from which he therefore had a
lucky escape.

The terrified, partly dressed Cumpstons, upon jumping out of their bedroom window twelve feet to the ground, fled for safety to the railway station and rushed into the night superintendent's office, screaming 'Murder!' They gasped out that they had 'escaped from a den of rogues and thieves', said that they thought they were being followed, and asked the startled night superintendent to search the waiting-room for them. When he had established that it was empty, the Cumpstons thankfully seated themselves in it, and he went off to call the police.

The police had no choice but to arrest the Cumpstons, who had disturbed everybody in the hotel with their frightened cries and pistol shots. They appeared in court the next day, charged with disorderly conduct, although when they told their story, insisted that they had not been drinking, and had summoned a friend from Gloucester by telegraph to vouch for their good characters, they were let off without a fine. The police inspected their room at the hotel, and *The Bristol Daily Post* reporter concluded his article, which was echoed in *The Times*, by saying 'from enquiries we have made of the police who examined the room at the Victoria Hotel occupied by the parties, there seems nothing whatever to warrant such conduct on their part. There is little doubt that the whole was an hallucination.'

But something very strange did happen to the unsuspecting Cumpstons, which frightened them to such an extent that they risked serious injury by jumping from a window placed twelve feet above the ground, in order to escape from their room. It is so inexplicable that we perhaps cannot blame the newspaper reporter for describing it as 'an hallucination'. By making the incident a mental aberration, neither he nor anyone else was required to face the possibility that the solid and familiar world of everyday experience might not be so solid or familiar after all.

Elizabeth Shaw of the Bristol Central Library tells me that the Victoria Hotel stood at 140 Thomas Street, Bristol, although its name was changed to the Bute Arms in 1876. Its proprietor at the time of the Cumpston incident was a Josiah Brown. The hotel was demolished in the mid-1920s. The Bristol and Exeter railway station to which the Cumpstons ran is today called Temple Meads.

The 1871 census returns do not record the Cumpstons as living in Virginia Road, Leeds, but they were residents there at the time of the 1881 census, occupying Number 35, which means that they must have been relatively new arrivals in the road when they had their frightening experience in 1873. Yet this neither halted Thomas Cumpston's rise in the world – his occupation in 1881 was given as a 'linen manufacturer employing about 90 persons' – nor Annie Cumpston's capacity to have children: she had three, two boys and a girl, between 1876 and 1879. The 1881 census returns also record that the Cumpstons then employed three domestic servants; a cook, a housemaid, and a nurse. They were, in other words, people of some substance.

A quite different disappearance occurred just over a quarter of a century later, on a remote and tiny Scottish Island named Eilean More, one of the seven Flannan Islands which lie fifteen miles west of Lewis, out in the Atlantic. A lighthouse on the island, whose construction was begun in 1895, was finally completed in December 1899, and it was exactly one year later that the entire lighthouse crew of three, namely lighthouse-keeper James Ducat, assistant keeper Thomas Marshall, and occasional keeper Donald McArthur, vanished without trace and have never been seen again.

The first indication that all was not as it should be on Eilean More came when the lighthouse failed to illuminate on the night of Saturday 15 December 1900, and anxiety about the safety of the men there grew when the lighthouse subsequently remained out of service. There were no radios in those days and an investigation could only be carried out by sending a boat to the rock. But unfortunately, it proved impossible to do this right away because of the very bad weather.

Indeed, it wasn't until 26 December that the Northern Lighthouse Board steamer *Hesperus* managed to dock at Eilean More. Aboard was the relieving lighthouse-keeper Joseph Moore, who climbed on to the rock with two seamen from the vessel. They found that the lighthouse quarters were quite empty, but chores, such as bed-making and priming the lamps, had been done. The last entry on the record slate had been made by James Ducat at 9 a.m. on 15 December, which indicates that he and the others disappeared sometime later that day before the lamps could be lit.

The only articles of equipment missing were the oilskins and seaboots belonging to Ducat and Marshall, and a tool-chest that was normally stored in a crevice about one hundred feet above one of the two jetties. However, because oilskins and seaboots were only worn by the men when they went on to the jetties, these missing articles seemed to suggest that Ducat and Marshall had perhaps been swept away by a sudden large wave while outside, and that McArthur, running down to the jetty to throw them a lifebelt, had been washed away too.

Yet this seemingly plausible explanation was rejected when it was realized that the weather on 15 December had been calm and mild, the bad weather not beginning until the 16th. Even if one of the men had accidentally slipped into the sea and had perhaps been knocked unconscious, only one of the remaining two men would have jumped in after him. Or if there had been some freak tide, which might have suddenly risen and covered the jetty and pulled anyone on it into the sea, it is most unlikely that all three crewmen would have been outside at the same time, especially one not wearing his oilskins and seaboots.

Some accounts state that a half-eaten meal of salted mutton and boiled potatoes was found on the kitchen table, and that one of the chairs was lying on its side. If true, this would pinpoint the men's disappearance to lunch-time of 15 December. We cannot of course know what happened to them, but it is possible that the mystery of their disappearance, especially when it is remembered that none of their bodies was ever found, could be the result of some supernatural event, which whisked them out of our world as soon as 'the lamp was trimmed, the oil fountains and canteens were filled up, and the lens and machinery cleaned' (from the official report).

These four cases are very different in how and where they occurred, which makes one wonder if the people themselves unwittingly did anything to precipitate their (or their room's) vanishing or if they were simply unlucky victims of some strange split in the fabric of our world?

Yet there is one factor common to them all, which is that they occurred in a place other than their own home. Diderici was in prison, 'Lucy Lightfoot' was visiting a local church, the Cumpstons were staying overnight at a strange hotel, and the keepers were all in residence at their remote lighthouse. Similarly, if you look back over the many cases involving vanishing people that I have discussed so far, it will be found that none of those who disappeared did so when they were at home. This is true even of Owen Parfitt, who vanished outside his cottage, and of Peter

Williamson. Most disappearants, in fact, were at another place, in another town, or in another country, at the time of their exit from the world.

I shall end this chapter by considering a number of supernatural disappearances which have been reported by witnesses who happened to be nearby when the person concerned vanished. Such intimate views of one of life's greatest mysteries are, perhaps not surprisingly, rare. They bring us as close as we can reasonably hope to get to the moment when the 'impossible' becomes an actuality!

The first case is extremely strange. It involves a medium, part of whom, namely her legs, disappeared at a seance. The rest of her body remained solid and quite unaffected by the vanishing of her limbs. Fortunately these soon rematerialized, enabling her to walk away from the chair on which she had been sitting.

The seance took place at Helsingfors, Finland, on 11 December 1893, in the home of a professional engineer named Seiling. The medium was Madame d'Esperance. Fifteen well-educated, middle-class adults, three of whom were army generals, formed the circle, and one of them, Vera Hjelt, a school headmistress, later described what happened in a letter she wrote to Professor M.A. Aksakov. The latter included it, along with other first-hand testimonies, in his book about the affair, which was published in France in 1896 under the title *Un Case de Dematerialisation Partielle du Corps d'un Medium* – and which, the author observes, 'throws a living light on the mysterious phenomenon of materialization'.

'Madame d'Esperance' was the pseudonym of Elizabeth Hope (1855–1919), or more accurately it is the French translation of her surname. She was English by birth, and in due course she became one of the most famous materialization mediums of her time. She had the ability or 'power' to cause spirits to manifest as luminous phantoms in the darkness of seance rooms. To accomplish this she worked with a curtained cabinet or closet, several feet in height, within which the spirit would materialize before emerging from it to stand alongside herself.

The 'circle' of persons assembled in the dining-room of Mr Seiling was actually oval in shape, at one end of which sat the medium, with her curtained cabinet standing behind her. The room was lit by a shaded light placed in one corner, which cast a dull glow over the scene. There was no table or other obstacle between the medium and her sitters.

I was the third person on the right of the medium [explains Mrs Hjelt]. This place was very advantageous. I had the medium in front of me, at an angle of 45 degrees, and the upper part of her body was distinctly outlined in semi-profile on the window-blind, which hung down from one of the room's windows. I was so near to her that I was able to see her clothes clearly, her hands, and her feet crossed and placed in front of her. I was therefore able, by bending and leaning forwards a little, to see the very least of her movements.

Madame d'Esperance had little trouble in producing effects once the seance began; she did not even have to go into a trance. Quite soon a 'spirit' arm was thrust out from the cabinet behind her, holding a gauze-like cloth. When this withdrew, it was quickly replaced by a 'luminous apparition' which emerged from the cabinet and clasped a hand of the nearest sitter. The apparition was then given a pair of scissors by Mr Seiling, who asked it to cut a piece from the previously displayed gauze, and give it to him. This the apparition did. Afterwards it was given a pencil and a piece of paper by another sitter, which enabled it to write, lightly and rapidly, a message in Swedish for him. The recipient placed the paper in his pocket without revealing what it said. It was after this that the lower extremities of the medium vanished.

Moments later, her hands again fell to her knees [continues Vera Hjelt]. I then saw her again try to put her hands on her knees, and I noticed that she became more and more agitated. This seemed curious to me. I leaned further forward ... the medium then let out a huge sigh which made one imagine some very disagreeable sensations. Several seconds later, she said to her neighbour on the left, Mr Seiling, 'Give me your hand.' – Mr Seiling lifted his hand and put it out. She then said, 'Touch me here!' – Mr Seiling responded: 'It's extraordinary, I see Madame d'Esperance and I hear her speak, but when I feel her chair I find nothing; she is not there; there is nothing there but her dress!' His touch seemed to produce a sadness in the medium.

None the less, Madame d'Esperance brought forward five other sitters in turn to verify what Mr Seiling had noticed, one of whose hands she took in her own and guided them down her body until they suddenly came in contact with the chair. The man exclaimed his surprise several times at this. Each investigation appeared to cause the medium great discomfort, and on two occasions she had to ask for a drink of water.

Someone suggested that they should perhaps end the seance at that point, but this was rejected until the legs of the medium had returned. Fortunately this soon happened.

> Without there being the least movement of her dress [says the stunned but watchful Mrs Hjelt], I heard the medium say, 'That's better already,' then several moments later, she said energetically, 'Look here at them!' As for the pleats of her dress, I saw them fill out, and without knowing how, the end of her feet reappeared crossed as they had been before the phenomenon.
>
> In order to assure myself that I had a lucid mind in making all these observations I have just related to you, I attempted to detach my thoughts from everything that happened around me and to fix them on something indifferent and unrelated to the seance. I tried to see if my thoughts obeyed my will. I was perfectly reassured of that. By virtue of the fact, I therefore dare to affirm that the phenomena ... were effectively produced, and that the medium made no movement to contribute to the appearance or disappearance of the said phenomena.

In other words, and this was vouched for by the other sitters at that remarkable seance, the disappearance of Madame d'Esperance's legs actually took place, at least so far as could be humanly judged (not forgetting that in Victorian times one was not allowed to lift a woman's dress to look underneath it). Their unexpected loss certainly alarmed the medium, who was doubtless relieved that such a disturbing occurrence never happened to her again.

It has of course been suggested by sceptics that Madame d'Esperance somehow manipulated her legs to give the impression that they had vanished, or had placed them in a hole cut in the top of the chair to render them invisible. These objections, however, are nullified by the close watch kept by Vera Hjelt upon the medium, who saw no movement of her legs or lifting up of her body, which would necessarily have occurred to bring about such a deception. The chair in which she sat was a stuffed one with a stuffed back, and no aperture was detected in its top to allow Madame d'Esperance's legs to be secreted within it. Anyway, such a deception would have required the active collusion of Mr Seiling, at whose house the seance occurred. There is no evidence for this. However, I must point out that because a 'luminous apparition' made an appearance immediately before Madame d'Esperance's legs vanished, it might possibly have distracted the attention of even the watchful Mrs Hjelt enough to make her miss any suspicious movement on the part of Madame d'Esperance.

The next witnessed supernatural disappearance I want to mention took place on stage at a public theatre in New York. The person who vanished was a magician named William Neff, although it was not part of his stage act. Rather, it was a spontaneous happening of which he was not aware, and which was as puzzling to him as it was to those who literally saw through him.

The incident occurred one wet Saturday afternoon at the Paramount Theatre, when Neff was working his way through his stage routine. There were only a few people in the audience, yet one of them was Neff's close friend, the highly respected New York all-night radio host Long John Nebel (1912–1978), who later wrote up what he saw.

According to Nebel, as he watched the magician's performance, 'it seemed that Neff's body was becoming minutely translucent', a process that continued until 'you could see the traveller curtain clearly behind this transparent figure'. But despite Neff's form completely vanishing from sight, his voice could still be heard talking 'patter' by the stunned onlookers, which suggested to Nebel that Neff was not aware of what had taken place. Then 'gradually a rather faint outline, like a very fine pencil sketch of Neff, appeared again', which was filled in until the magician became completely reconstituted.

Nebel went backstage immediately after the show and questioned Neff closely about his disappearance. He learned that it was not a trick and that Neff had experienced the phenomenon twice before, once when he was performing his act on stage in Chicago, the other time when he was at home with his wife, who was reduced to a state of acute shock by his sudden fading away. What is particularly curious about all three incidents is that Neff claimed he did not feel any difference within himself as he vanished, which presumably explains why he did not know that anything odd had happened to him until the reaction of witnesses told him otherwise.

William Neff's easy and unrecognized (by him) fading of form contrasts with the disagreeable effect that the vanishing of her legs had upon Madame d'Esperance. We can only wonder what the reason for this might be. Yet neither case, remarkable though both are, can compare with the astonishing disappearances of Jean Durrant, who was able to vanish at will. Equally incredibly, his disappearances were accompanied by the teleportation of his body out of any room in which he had been locked.

Jean Durrant, a French-Canadian, first came to public attention in 1898, when he told a Winnipeg doctor about his strange power over himself. He was then twenty-four years old. The doctor, whose name has not been recorded, was not impressed by his claims, thinking that they were quite impossible, even nonsensical. But Durrant was insistent.

'I tell you again – I assure you – I can dissolve my body when and where I please,' he said quietly. 'I don't attempt to explain it. I simply will myself to dissolve, and then I know absolutely nothing until I'm normal again. Why, I can prove it!'

The doctor shrugged, thinking the man was mad. But the proof of the pudding is in the eating. He invited Durrant to demonstrate his remarkable gift then and there.

This brought some protest from Durrant, who claimed that he found it difficult to disappear while he was being watched. Watching eyes, he said, somehow robbed him of the power, although he had once managed to disappear in front of another person, a man from Toronto named Williams, yet the experience had made him ill. But if the doctor cared to tie him up and lock him away, he would extricate himself in moments. The doctor shrugged, supposing that he was simply an escapologist like Houdini. Then he remembered his little dispensing room. It only had a door and one tiny window, which was far too small for a human body to squeeze through.

'Now if you can get out of that,' mumbled the doctor, chuckling awkwardly, 'then I'll believe you.'

Durrant threw off his clothes and stepped willingly into the cubicle-like room. The doctor locked him in, put the key in his pocket, and stood back to keep a careful eye on the door. It wasn't long before he heard the sound of deep breathing from within the room. Then, suddenly, there was nothing. He waited tensely, wondering what would happen next.

A voice sounded at his elbow, making him jump.

'Well, are you satisfied now?' Durrant said.

The doctor swung around and stared incredulously at the man, who stood behind him as naked as the day that he was born. The man was out and free. He had achieved the impossible!

The successful conclusion to this test had the physician contacting two of his medical colleagues. He asked them to repeat his experiment to verify Durrant's amazing power and to see if they could work out how such a thing could be done. His colleagues did as he requested, and Durrant astounded them by easily and quickly appearing outside the rooms in which they bound and locked him. Yet neither doctor was able to explain what had happened. Eyewitness testimony of Durrant's power to disappear at will was next sought from Mr Williams of Toronto, who swore on oath that he had watched as the man faded from view before him, his dressing-gown falling to the floor as he disappeared.

This led to the doctors and a group of their friends asking Durrant if he would be willing to undergo a rigorous test performed by the police. It was necessary, they said, to absolutely assure themselves that his disappearances were genuine. Durrant shrugged his shoulders but immediately agreed. The police were sceptical but obliging, and at the police station Durrant was stripped and closely searched for any lock-picking device. None was found. He was then placed in a cell, bound by the wrists and ankles, and locked in. Six policemen stood outside the cell, watching the door. Jean Durrant did not come through it. Yet two or three minutes after he had been imprisoned he walked round the corner of the corridor in which they were standing, still naked but otherwise solid and unscathed. He had once again confounded all concerned!

Another test was held by the police, one more foolproof than before. This time his naked body was secured at the wrists and ankles with handcuffs, and he was further restrained by being chained to the cell wall. The cell door was locked and afterwards sealed at several points with wax. Witnesses again stood outside to watch for some miracle of escapalogy, yet not one saw Jean Durrant come through it.

But none the less, he appeared suddenly in the corridor again, taking less time to join those waiting for him than before. When the cell was opened the wax seals were undamaged, and the handcuffs and chain manacles were found to be still locked closed.

Each of these tests held in Winnipeg seemed to completely vindicate Jean Durrant's claim that he could make himself disappear. The man was a walking marvel, the impossible made possible. He could make himself vanish and reappear elsewhere simply by willing it to happen. But it wasn't long before he apparently came unstuck.

An invitation from interested parties in Chicago, USA, requested him to submit to a similar test organized by the police there. Jean Durrant accepted the challenge and travelled to the Windy City. At the police station he was again searched and secured as before, and the heavy cell door was closed upon him. But there was no sign of him after half an hour, and when one hour had gone by the watching policemen were sure that he was a charlatan. The cell door was opened by the scoffers – who were astonished to discover that it was quite empty, the handcuffs and chain lying upon its floor!

Jean Durrant was never seen or heard of again. No one knows to this day what became of that amazing young man. Did he reappear outside the prison and simply walk away, naked and unashamed, into the night? Or did he, as perhaps seems more likely, vanish from the police cell and get trapped in the invisible dimension, lost in a world more remote from ours than the other side of the moon?

The last three cases are sufficiently different from those previously discussed to be legitimately termed 'varieties' of supernatural disappearance. They in fact form a curious progression, which starts with the isolated and involuntary vanishing of a body part (Madame d'Esperance's legs), moves on to the infrequent and involuntary disappearance of the whole body (William Neff), and ends with the as frequently as desired voluntary disappearance of the whole body (Jean Durrant). The first and second took place in full view of several witnesses, whose very presence seemed to encourage the phenomenon, whereas the voluntary disappearances of Jean Durrant were inhibited by even one pair of watching eyes, although the simple proximity of human beings who could not see what was going on did not lessen his power to vanish.

None of the people concerned were unusually frightened or distressed in any way before they either partially or completely disappeared, which reveals that negative emotions did not play a precipitative role in what happened to them. Nor were any suffering from the threat of violence. And with the exception of the disappearance of 'Lucy Lightfoot', there were no exceptional atmospheric or astronomical conditions which might have caused the phonemonon. Indeed, Jean Durrant could vanish at will, whatever the circumstances, except when robbed of his power by onlookers.

9 Can Such Things Really Be?

You may wander for years through literary circles and never meet anybody who has heard of Ambrose Bierce; and then you may hear some erudite student whisper in an awed voice: 'Bierce is the greatest living prose writer.'

Arnold Bennett

In 1893 a book about ghostly appearances and other supernatural happenings, entitled *Can Such Things Be?*, was published in the United States. Its contents are presented as true accounts, which had apparently been gathered by or told to its author, the well-known American journalist Ambrose Gwinnett Bierce. Towards the end of the book, running consecutively, are found three dramatic supernatural disappearances, which are followed by a quite detailed consideration of what might have caused them, a discussion which includes reference to the 'distinguished scientist' Dr Hern of Leipsic (sic), who apparently believed that our visible world contains mysterious vacua or void places, rather like holes in a Swiss cheese, which are openings into the invisible world and through which the occasional unlucky individual may fall, and so disappear.

The three accounts mentioned below are all classics of their kind. Two of them, namely *The Difficulty of Crossing a Field* and *Charles Ashmore's Trail*, occurred (or are set) in the United States, and the third, *An Unfinished Race*, took place (or is set) in England. The two American stories are unusual in that they acquired an 'afterlife' of their own, having given rise by some as yet unexplained process to identical stories which are located in different places. This has caused much confusion among writers about mysterious disappearances, who have all too frequently

129

presented one or other of the latter as the original and 'true' story, without realizing that they were dealing in second-hand goods. As we shall see, the ersatz stories all take place at a different date from the original, and that as the number of years increase between them and their source, so the new story is placed further and further away geographically!

The original stories are given a special poignancy by the fact that Bierce himself mysteriously vanished in 1913. Indeed, no one knows to this day what became of him. And because Bierce disappeared without trace, like James Worson in *An Unifinished Race*, it is just possible that our cantankerous writer may have stepped into one of Dr Hern's vacua himself!

Since *An Unfinished Race* is the shortest and least well-known of the three, I shall reproduce it in its entirety. I think the reader will agree that it is an astonishing tale:

James Burne Worson was a shoe-maker who lived in Leamington, Warwickshire, England. He had a little shop in one of the by-ways leading off the road to Warwick. In his humble sphere he was esteemed an honest man, although like many of his class in English towns he was somewhat addicted to drink. When in liquor he would make foolish wagers. On one of these too frequent occasions he was boasting of his prowess as a pedestrian and athlete, and the outcome was a match against nature. For the sake of one sovereign he undertook to run all the way to Coventry and back, a distance of something more than forty miles. This was on the 3rd day of September in 1873. He set out at once, the man with whom he had made the bet – whose name is not remembered – accompanied by Barham Wise, a linen draper, and Hamerson Burns, a photographer, I think, following in a light cart or wagon.

For several miles, Worson went on very well, at an easy gait, without apparent fatigue, for he had really great powers of endurance and was not sufficiently intoxicated to enfeeble them. The three men in the wagon kept a short distance in the rear, giving him occasional friendly 'chaff' or encouragement, as the spirit moved them. Suddenly – in the very middle of the roadway, not a dozen yards from them, and with their eyes full upon him – the man seemed to stumble, pitched headlong forward, uttered a terrible cry and vanished! He did not fall to the earth – he vanished before touching it. No trace of him was ever discovered.

After remaining at and about the spot for some time, with aimless irresolution, the three men returned to Leamington, told their astonishing story and were afterwards taken into custody. But they were of good standing, had always been considered truthful, were sober at the time of the occurrence, and nothing ever transpired to discredit their sworn account of their extraordinary adventure, concerning the truth of which, nevertheless, public opinion was divided, throughout the United Kingdom. If they had something to conceal, their choice of means is certainly one of the most amazing ever made by sane human beings.

But while the account is persuasive, how true is it?

The perceptive reader might have noticed a couple of problems with it straight away. For one thing, the return distance between Leamington and Coventry, which is given as 'something more than forty miles', is actually less than half that. Then there are the names of the people concerned: 'James Burne Worson', 'Barham Wise', and 'Hamerson Burns' all sound suspiciously American, although 'Wise' is a local name and PC Joe Poland of the Warwickshire police tells me that 'Hamerson' is a north of England Christian name. However, I'm more troubled by the surname 'Worson', Not only had I never heard of it before I read Bierce's story, but I have since been unable to locate it in any reference book of British surnames. It isn't, it seems, known in this country.

I then became curious as to how Ambrose Bierce, who was based for much of his life in San Francisco, in the far west of the United States, came to hear about something that apparently happened just outside Leamington Spa, of all places? This was explained when I discovered, to my surprise, that Bierce, an evident anglophile, had not only lived and worked in England between July 1872 and late August 1875, but that he had resided with his wife and first-born son at 20 South Parade, Leamington Spa, from the spring of 1874 until August 1875. Indeed, Ambrose Bierce's second son, Leigh, was born at Leamington in May 1874! So far as I can ascertain, during September 1873, when the Worson disappearance reportedly happened, Bierce was living temporarily in Hampstead, London, following several months spent in Bath. Hence he might have read about the Worson disappearance in the national newspapers, and/or he might have heard about it by word of mouth when he lived at Leamington.

But although Bierce was therefore admirably positioned to pick up reports of a strange disappearance occurring outside Leamington Spa, it has proved impossible to locate any information that might substantiate his remarkable story. The most depressing loss in this regard are the case records of the then independent Leamington Spa Borough Police Force (it was amalgamated with Warwickshire Constabulary in 1947), all of which have been destroyed by official vandals. This means that the details of Worson's disappearance as described by his friends to the police, if such interviews ever took place, can never be re-examined. But Commander Terence Gardner, who has a wide knowledge of and deep interest in the history of Leamington, has found no reference to the incident in either his own notes or his books about the town.

And unfortunately, my search through every edition of *The Royal Leamington Spa Courier* newspaper printed in 1873 has revealed no report of the Worson disappearance. Likewise, there was no mention of it in *The Times*, despite the paper reporting, in its 11 December 1873 issue, the strange incident involving the Cumpstons at Bristol. None of the Leamington Spa trade directories of the 1870s list shoemaker James Worson, linen draper Barham Wise, or photographer Hamerson Burns, or indeed mention any of these names in association with different occupations, although I agree that it is only implied by Bierce, not stated, that Wise and Burns lived and worked in the town. Similarly, the 1868 *Leamington Post Office Directory*, the closest I could find to the date in question, contains none of these names.

This naturally suggests either a) that Bierce, writing some twenty years after the event, got his dates wrong, or b) that he is presenting a piece of fiction as a true narrative. As no one has ever come across such a remarkable disappearance in the newspapers of another year or even sited at another place, it may mean that the latter alternative is true.

Who then was Ambrose Gwinnett Bierce, or Almighty God Bierce as some called him, and what is his track record for truth?

Bierce was one of America's native proletarian writers, having been born at his parents' farm in Meigs County, Ohio, on 24 June 1842. His formal education was virtually non-existent, and his first paid job, which he started soon after his family moved to Elkhart, Indiana, was as a labourer at the town's brick yard. He later became a waiter. Bierce never grew above 5'4'' in height, and he developed many of the personality characteristics associated with the undersized: tetchiness, over-sensitivity, pushiness, and ambition.

Yet significantly, when he was fifteen years of age Bierce began an intimate affair with a 70-year-old Elkhart matron, although who seduced whom is not recorded. The relationship continued, albeit surreptitiously, for several years, and it was a liaison that gave the archetypal toy boy the idea that he might achieve more in life than waiting at tables. His elderly lover encouraged him to read and to write, discussed literature with him, and fired his enthusiasm for the printed word. She pointed him in the right direction, and he took the road he was shown.

His life underwent its next momentous change, as it did for so many Americans, when the Civil War broke out in 1861. He enlisted for the Union in the Indiana Volunteers, and fought with them throughout the war, surviving serious injury and numerous battles. In fact the war was the best period of his life; he not only looked back at it nostalgically in later years, but it provided him with a setting for some of his most effective and powerful stories. After the war Bierce went west and settled in San Francisco, where he became a full-time journalist, eventually maturing into the acclaimed and acerbic columnist of such prominent West Coast newspapers as *The San Francisco News, The Argonaut,* the *San Francisco Examiner*, and *The Cosmopolitan*. He also wrote a number of books, several of them collections of short stories, whose titles often reflect the supernatural interests and odd humour of the man, such as *The Fiend's Delight* (1872), *Cobwebs from an Empty Skull* (1874), and *The Devil's Dictionary* (1906). The short stories comprising *In the Midst of Life* (1892), which are set in the Civil War, include one of his best known, *An Occurrence at Owl Creek Bridge*, which has been made into a film.

But truthfulness, except perhaps in an artistic sense, was never one of Bierce's strong points. He was 'economical' in this regard whenever it suited him. He told everybody, for example, that he had worked on his parents' farm until he was seventeen years old, when he ran away to Chicago to become a freelance journalist, a job he continued until the start of the Civil War. He claimed a knowledge of many foreign languages, and pretended to possess a deep understanding of Greek, Latin, French, and German, whereas in reality his grasp of languages was rudimentary. He likewise gave the impression that he was *au fait* not only with the great works of literature, but with philosophical ideas, political movements, world trends and events, art and music, and a host of other matters, that were, as often as not, quite foreign to him. 'Bierce,' says one of his biographers, 'was beset by a false sense of educational deficiency. Always he was either consciously or unconsciously on the defensive, fearing ridicule.' He was, in other words, neither a happy nor a truthful man.

Let us then only briefly examine the disappearances described in *The Difficulty of Crossing a Field* and *Charles Ashmore's Trail*. They are fascinating stories, but unfortunately I have likewise found nothing definite to substantiate them. Hence they are probably fictitious, the product of Bierce's remarkable imagination, although like all good mysteries, there is room for doubt.

The Difficulty of Crossing a Field begins:

> One morning in July, 1854, a planter named Williamson, living six miles from Selma, Alabama, was sitting with his wife and child on the veranda of his dwelling. Immediately in front of the house was a lawn, perhaps fifty yards in extent between the house and the public road, or, as it was called, the 'pike'. Beyond this road lay a close-cropped pasture of some ten acres, level and without a tree, rock, or any natural or artificial object on its surface. At the time there was not even a domestic animal in the field. In another field, beyond the pasture, a dozen slaves were at work under an overseer.

The story continues with Mr Williamson rising from his seat, informing his wife that he has forgotten to tell the overseer about 'those horses', and walking towards, and then across, the pasture field. As he enters the field he is passed by a neighbour, Armour Wren, riding along the 'pike' in his open carriage, driven by a coachman and accompanied by his son James and a negro boy. Armour Wren suddenly remembers he must tell Williamson that he can't deliver the horses he promised to bring him until the morrow.

The coachman was directed to drive back, and as the vehicle turned Williamson was seen by all three, walking leisurely across the pasture. At that moment one of the coach horses stumbled and came near to falling. It had no more than fairly recovered itself when James Wren cried: 'Why, father, what has become of Mr Williamson?'

Although none of the people in the carriage actually saw Williamson disappear, their attention having been momentarily distracted by the stumbling horse, all were conscious of the fact that he vanished from sight in the few seconds that they looked away. Armour Wren, according to Ambrose Bierce, when later testifying at the legal proceedings relating to the Williamson estate, said of the moment:

My son's examination caused me to look towards the spot where I had seen the deceased [sic] an instant before, but he was not there, nor was he anywhere visible ... Mrs Williamson, with her child in her arms and followed by several servants, came running down the walk in great excitement, crying: 'He is gone, he is gone! O God! What an awful thing!' and many other such exclamations, which I do not distinctly recollect ... Her manner was wild, but not more so, I think, than was natural under the circumstances. I have no reason to think she had at that time lost her mind. I have never since seen nor heard of Mr Williamson.

Ambrose Bierce rather strangely omits to give the Christian name of Williamson, yet has no difficulty in 'discovering' those of Wren and his son. Yet despite his omission, and notwithstanding the fact that his account is the first known description of the disappearance, later writers, although without explaining how they know, have claimed 'Orion' to be the forename of the missing man.

They have also claimed that 'the young' Ambrose Bierce personally investigated this remarkable mystery. But this is as unlikely as it is implausible. Not only was Bierce a bare fourteen years old when Williamson reputedly disappeared, but Selma was in those days a mere village, connected to the outside world by nothing more than dirt roads. In 1846 there was only one stretch of railroad in the whole of Alabama, and this ran between the townships of Montgomery and Cheham, coming no closer than thirty-five miles to Selma. A railroad to the town was not constructed until several years afterwards. And in 1854 the Bierce family was living at Elkhart, Indiana, far away to the north. Indeed, Bierce might as well have been living on another planet for the time and trouble it would have taken him to get to Selma, not to mention the expense.

But just as strangely, an article appeared in a 1953 issue of *Fate* magazine entitled 'How Lost Was My Father?' by writer Stuart Palmer, which described an almost identical disappearance that supposedly took place outside the town of Gallatin, Tennessee, on 23 September 1880. The farmer that supernaturally disappears is called David Lang. He leaves his wife (named Emma) and the two children (Sarah and George) on the porch of their farmhouse, to walk across a 40-acre field to inspect the horses in an adjacent paddock. As he strides across the field he is noticed by two friends, Judge August Peck and his brother-in-law Wade, who are driving in their open buggy to visit him. They both wave at Lang, who, seeing them, responds to their wave and turns back towards the farmhouse, when all of a sudden he vanishes from sight, never to be seen again.

Palmer claimed he heard the story from Sarah Lang, the daughter of David Lang. But it is of course Bierce's story set in another place and at a different date, with its characters given different names. Yet Bierce's 'Armour Wren' is immediately recognizable as Palmer's 'August Peck', whose surname surely derives from the tongue-in-cheek association of 'a wren is a bird, and birds peck'! More significantly, I have carefully examined an 1878 map of Gallatin and area. which gives the names of all the farmers and landholders, but found no David Lang, or any other Lang, shown; and I understand that the 1880 census records of Sumner county, wherein Gallatin lies, have likewise been examined with a similar lack of success.

However, Stuart Palmer, not content with plagiarizing one of Bierce's stories, performs the same act on *Charles Ashmore's Trail*, which provided him with the original of the addendum outlined below:

In August 1881, about one year after the disappearance of David Lang, according to Palmer, his two children, Sarah and George, walked across the 40-acre field and noticed a ring of stunted yellow grass at the place where their father had vanished.

Sarah instinctively called out to him, and, to her astonishment, she heard him reply in a disembodied voice, repeatedly pleading for help. But there was nothing the children could do but listen, with tears rolling down their faces. Their mother hurried to the spot on being told of what had occurred, and she also heard her husband's voice. The phenomenon continued for several days, the voice growing increasingly fainter, until at last it was heard no more.

The story made another jump in space and time not long after, when it was reported in the *New York Sun* that on 23 April 1885, a farmer named Isaac Martin, of Salem, Virginia, had also walked into a field and disappeared, although exactly who witnessed his going was not recorded.

After having moved north from Alabama to Tennessee, then east to Virginia, the next logical move for any travelling story is to cross the Atlantic and try its luck in England. Now I don't wish to appear unduly sceptical, but it is perhaps pushing coincidence too far, knowing that 'Orion' Williamson reputedly vanished in a field watched by his wife and child in July 1854, to accept entirely without question that Peter Williamson likewise disappeared in his garden watched by his wife and two children in July 1974. The similarity of names and dates is very suspicious. I want to ask, with apologies to Charles Fort, 'was somebody collecting Williamsons?'

I came across the Peter Williamson disappearance in a book entitled *Encounters with the Unknown*, which was published by Robert Hale in 1990. I was unhappy with the fact that author Colin Parsons, while stating that the Williamson family live in Somerset, does not reveal exactly where, although I presumed this was because the family, whom Parsons says he interviewed, did not wish to be hounded by cranks and oddballs. I therefore set to work examining Somerset newspapers published around the time of the disappearance, in the hope of learning more, but was unable to find any reference to it in them. I next wrote to Colin Parsons, via his publisher, asking what was the reason for this, but the letter was returned along with the unhappy news that Colin Parsons had died. I can only hope that the deceased author did not imitate Stuart Palmer, but the lack of any supporting evidence leaves it open to question.

The third Ambrose Bierce story, entitled *Charles Ashmore's Trail*, records the disappearance of 16-year-old Charles Ashmore on 9 November 1878, with the same attention to detail and air of truthful reportage that distinguish the other two. This time the mysterious event takes place at Quincy, Illinois, where the Ashmore family have a farm. Some distance away from their farmhouse lies a clear spring, from which they obtain their household water. At about nine o'clock on the night in question, Charles Ashmore takes a tin bucket and goes to the well, but does not return. Eventually his father, Christian Ashmore, and his sister, Martha, take a lantern and go in search of him:

> A light snow had fallen, obliterating the path, but making the young man's trail conspicuous; each footprint was plainly defined. After going a little more than half-way – perhaps seventy-five yards – the father, who was in advance, halted, and elevating his lantern stood peering intently into the darkness ahead.
> 'What is the matter, father?' the girl asked.
> This was the matter: the trail of the young man had abruptly ended, and all beyond was smooth unbroken snow. The last footprints were as conspicuous as any in the line; the very nail-marks were distinctly visible ... The morning light showed nothing more. Smooth, spotless, unbroken, the shallow snow lay everwhere.

Charles Ashmore had disappeared, never to be seen again. Yet he was heard again. Four days later his grieving mother went to the spring for water, and as she passed the place where her son had vanished she heard his voice, coming first from one direction, then from another. She followed it until, exhausted by never being able to find the spot from whence it originated, she returned home.

> Questioned as to what the voice had said, she was unable to tell, yet averred that the words were perfectly distinct. In a moment the entire family was at the place, but nothing was heard, and the voice was believed to be an hallucination caused by the mother's great anxiety and her disordered nerves. But for months afterwards, at irregular intervals of a few days, the voice was heard by several members of the family, and by others. All declared it unmistakably the voice of Charles Ashmore; all agreed that it seemed to come from a great distance, faintly, yet with entire distinctness of articulation; yet none could determine its direction, nor repeat its words. The intervals of silence grew longer and

longer, the voice fainter and farther, and by midsummer it was heard no more.

We find in the mysterious voice, as I mentioned above, the source of Stuart Palmer's addendum to his version of the Orion Williamson story, for David Lang's children hear their father's voice at the spot where he vanished.

Charles Ashmore's Trail has spawned at least two derivatives, each with a corresponding change of date, place and people.

In the first repeat we move to Christmas Eve 1889; the place South Bend, Indiana. Eleven-year-old Oliver Larch goes to get a bucketful of water from the family well. Moments later his parents hear him cry, 'Help! They've got me!' They rush outside to find only his footprints in the snow, which end half-way to the well.

In the second, we find ourselves across the Atlantic at Rhayader, in Powys, Wales. It is now Christmas Eve 1909. Owen Thomas asks his 11-year-old son Oliver to fetch a bucket of water from the well in the yard. The boy goes willingly, but moments later is heard to cry, 'Help! Help! They've got me!' His parents dash outside, where once again they find nothing more than his footsteps in the snow, stopping half-way to the well. Young Oliver Thomas is neither seen nor heard of again.

Although both of these are obviously altered and transplanted versions of the Bierce story, I did write to Bryan Lawrence, the Local Studies Librarian at the County Library Headquarters, Llandrinod Wells, Powys, who once lived in Rhayader, to ask if anyone called Oliver Thomas had mysteriously vanished from Rhayader on or about the date mentioned. He replied somewhat wearily: 'This story has a habit of cropping up from time to time. It must be 10 years or more since I was last asked to verify [it]. At the time I checked all the available sources, including the local police, but was *unable to find any evidence that this event or any similar event ever happened in the locality*' (author's italics).

While I was waiting for Mr Lawrence's reply, I took the opportunity of checking to see if there was any snow on the ground in the Rhayader area on Friday 24 December 1909. What I found out was surprising, but it killed the idea of there being footprints in anybody's yard. *The Hereford Times* of Saturday 25 December 1909, recorded the previous week's weather. It began well enough:

Owing to the heavy snowfall on Saturday and Sunday, and also on Monday in many places, particularly in the North, outdoor work was suspended ... on Tuesday night, the weather continued cold, more snow fell; and this was followed on Wednesday morning by *a rapid thaw* [author's italics].

The idea of Charles Ashmore's footprints ending in the snow being taken as evidence for his supernatural disappearance is a neat one. It obviates the need for witnesses to his disappearance and gives an interesting twist to Bierce's third story which is supported by the disembodied voice, the latter reinforcing the message of gloom provided by the footprints.

But how original an idea is it? The answer to that is, not at all. Indeed, it was the absence of footprints in the snow which established that a genuine supernatural disappearance had happened over one thousand years before Ambrose Bierce was born, let alone put pen to paper.

The event is recorded in the Venerable Bede's *Life of St Cuthbert*. Cuthbert, a Northumbrian monk, was born about 634 and died in 687. While still quite a young man, he went to live at the monastery at Ripon, where he was appointed guestmaster. This required him to welcome and look after all who visited it.

Early one winter's morning, on going to the guest chamber, Cuthbert found a youth, who was a stranger to him, sitting within, whom he greeted warmly and on whom he performed the customary ablutions, notably the humble washing of his feet. Cuthbert presumed that the newcomer had walked through the snow all night to reach the monastery, which stood at an isolated spot, and told him that it would not be long before some food would be ready for him to eat. The youth thanked him, but said he was journeying to a distant place and must leave immediately if he was to reach his destination. Cuthbert begged him not to rush away, as he would surely faint with hunger in the snow. His protestations stayed the boy until a table was set and the food brought and put upon it. Cuthbert told him to eat and restore himself, then left him alone while he went to the bakery to fetch him some fresh bread.

When he came back the youth had vanished. The ground was covered with fresh snow but there were no footsteps to be seen. The man of God was amazed. He puzzled over what had happened and then went to put the table back in the storehouse. At the door there was a wonderfully fragrant odour. He looked about to see where it was coming from and there beside him were three loaves, unusually white and fine. Trembling he said to himself: 'Now I know that it was an angel, come not to be fed but to feed. He has brought bread such as cannot be produced on earth, whiter than the lily, sweeter than roses, more delicious than honey. Such food, it is obvious, comes not from this world of ours but from the paradise of joy. No wonder he refused human food when he can enjoy in Heaven the bread of eternal life.'

Despite Cuthbert's belief that his mysterious young visitor was an angel, we might take a more pragmatic view and agree that the marvel was not in his person but in his disappearance. For his sudden vanishing, if the evidence provided by the snow can be relied upon, seems to have been supernatural. However, if the three beautifully white loaves were really not the ones that Cuthbert brought back with him from the bakery – and the baking of white bread, as Cuthbert remarks, was quite impossible at such an early date – then they must have appeared supernaturally. And if there were really no footprints at all in the snow around the abbey, then the youth could not have arrived there by walking, which perhaps means that Cuthbert might have been right about where he came from after all!

A far more modern and often quoted disappearance has footsteps vanishing not in snow, but in sand. The incident which gave rise to this story took place in late July 1924, when two British airmen, Squadron Leader William Conway Day and his passenger Pilot Officer Donald Ramsey Stewart, of the No. 84 (Bombing) Squadron based at Shaibah, the airport for Basrah, Iraq, crash-landed their De Haviland plane eighteen miles south of the Basrah–Nasiriyeh railways line during a sandstorm. *The Times* of 31 July 1924, reported: 'The machine has since been found in a damaged condition, but despite a most careful search the officers have not been found. It is feared that they may have perished while endeavouring to reach the railway.'

Nobody knows to this day what happened to Squadron Leader Day or Pilot Officer Stewart, although Royal Air Force records do reveal that an armed desert patrol was sent in search of a raiding party of Arabs, who evidently removed items from the crashed plane and who may have encountered the two men and murdered them. However, it did not take long before someone, perhaps remembering the Bierce story, claimed that Day's and Stewart's footprints had been found in the sand leading away from their plane, and that, when followed, they came to a sudden and mysterious halt, while the men who made them were nowhere to be seen. Yet there is no evidence for such a remarkable exit from the world, which means that, despite the continuing mystery surrounding the fate of Bill Day and Donald Stewart, it is probable that their disappearance was in fact natural, not supernatural.

The disappearance of Ambrose Bierce in December 1913 is likewise a continuing mystery, for his body has also never been found. Yet his vanishing, as his friend and biographer Walter Neale observed, was an excellent career move: 'Nothing so augmented the interest in Ambrose Bierce as his disappearance. Obscurity is obscurity, but disappearance is fame.'

We know that Bierce left Washington by train on Thursday 2 October 1913, ostensibly heading for Mexico, where a civil war was in progress. He was seventy-one years old, a widower, in poor health (he was a chronic asthmatic), riven with nostalgia for the dear, dead and distant days of his life in the Indiana Volunteers, and bereft of the need or the inspiration to write. He had been talking about suicide for years to his close friends, assuring them that unless he died a natural death he would make away with himself soon after he reached the age of seventy.

> Within twelve months of his disappearance, one of his close associates, a young man ... while in Germany purchased a revolver as a present for Bierce [notes Walter Neale], which the latter said he would use when the time should come for him to blow out his brains. That would be the manner of his passing: a shot through the brain: that was the soldier's way, the decent method.

Bierce rode the train to Chickamauga, arriving there on 5 October; next he went to Murfreesboro, where he visited many old Civil War battlefields. Then he went on respectively to Nashville, Savannah, Shiloh, Corinth, and New Orleans. By 27 October he had reached San Antonio. In early November he was in Laredo, travelling from there to El Paso and then crossing the border into Mexico to reach Juarez, where he picked up his travelling papers. By 16 December 1913, he had stepped off the train at Chihuahua, where the last message of any kind was received from him. From there he steps into the unknown. The meeting he is said to have had with Pancho Villa is apocryphal. Walter Neale strongly denies that it ever took place: 'The absurdity of it! This old man, in his seventy-second year [sic], for many years a sufferer from asthma, had gone into the most asthmatic country in the world, there, on the flat alkali plains, to wheeze out his life!'

Although Bierce probably did not supernaturally disappear, but more likely shot himself in some remote gully, he came closest in his poetry – he was a fine poet – to expressing the essence of that strange dimension where those that have so mysteriously vanished may go. The following verses are from a poem called *The Passing Show*:

> I know not if it was a dream. I came
> Unto a land where something seemed the same
> That I had known as 'twere but yesterday,
> But what it was I could not rightly name.

> It was a strange and melancholy land,
> Silent and desolate. On either hand
> Lay waters of a sea that seemed as dead,
> And dead above it seemed the hills to stand.

So can such things as Ambrose Bierce described really be? Yes, they can, as I believe this book shows. It's just that Bierce accurately described the phenomenon without bothering to surround it with a verifiable framework of fact.

10   Vanishing Ships and Aircraft

Herewith the foresaid women vanished immediately out of
their sight. This was reputed at the first but some vain
fantastical illusion ... but afterwards the common opinion
was, that these women were either the weird sisters, that is
(as ye would say) the goddesses of destiny, or else some
nymphs or fairies, imbued with knowledge of prophecie by
their necromantical science, because everything came to pass
as they had spoken.

From the *Chronicle of England and Scotland* by Raphael
Holinshed

I have so far written mainly about the supernatural disappearance
of individual people, to a lesser extent about their sudden
appearance, the former often preceding the latter, and last of all
about the appearance and vanishing of animals and of objects. I
would now like to enlarge upon the last-named group by
considering some interesting cases of supernaturally disappearing
ships and planes, although these invariably vanish with a number
of people aboard – their crews and any passengers.

Writing about such ships and planes is fraught with difficulty,
however, because as both forms of conveyance operate in
potentially dangerous areas – the sea and the sky – it is often
impossible to distinguish between those which have disappeared
supernaturally and those whose vanishing has been brought about
by freak weather conditions, uncharted hazards, mechanical
failure, navigational error, human stupidity, and other natural
causes.

Hundreds of ships and other craft are lost, presumed sunk, each
year, which is why the unexplained disappearance of a small
number of them is perhaps to be expected. These are the vessels

that leave behind no survivors and no flotsam which can be positively identified as belonging to them, although the enormously large area of the seas and the oceans often makes searching for such evidence a hit-or-miss affair. In these cases the question therefore frequently arises: are the lost ships victims of the elements (or of some other natural cause) or have they been mysteriously snatched away from the world? The answer, however, is always uncertain. The best that can be said of them is: 'Missing without trace, cause of loss unknown.'

The type of marine disappearance which best captures the public's imagination is that involving the loss of the crew but not the vessel, the latter being found drifting empty and helpless. There are a number of intriguing cases of this type on record, the most famous being the disappearance of those aboard the *Mary Celeste*, yet none can be classified as supernatural because they are usually a number of other possible reasons why the crew and the passengers, if any, are no longer on board. You will remember, of course, that a supernatural disappearance can only be accepted as genuine if it is witnessed or if no other explanation will suffice.

The *Mary Celeste* mystery has frequently been written about, often by those who think they have solved it, yet a word or two more about the case will hopefully not try the reader's patience too much, as I only wish to show that although the disappearance of the people on board is still a puzzle, their loss was almost certainly not supernatural.

The American-owned *Mary Celeste*, skippered by Captain Benjamin Briggs and manned by a crew of seven, set sail from New York in the second week of November 1872, with a cargo of crude alcohol. Also aboard were Captain Briggs' wife Sarah and the couple's 2-year-old daughter Sophia. The ship left port at the same time as an English vessel, the *Dei Gratia*, whose skipper, Captain Morehouse, was a friend of Captain Briggs. The *Mary Celeste* was bound for Genoa, Italy, and the *Dei Gratia* for Gibraltar.

The American ship, being the faster of the two, soon pulled away from the *Dei Gratia*, whose crew lost sight of her until Thursday 5 December, when they found the *Mary Celeste* adrift in the mid-Atlantic. A boarding party quickly determined that she was devoid of life, and the ship's log revealed that she had been drifting for at least nine days. She was still entirely seaworthy, although there was quite a lot of water below decks.

Thus far the situation is very puzzling. Whatever could have happened to the nine adults and one child that were aboard the *Mary Celeste*? This question naturally preoccupied Captain Morehouse, who crewed the abandoned vessel from the *Dei Gratia* and sailed with her to Gibraltar, where an inquiry attempted to come up with an answer. After examining the evidence, those concerned concluded that a mutiny had taken place. However, one important clue to what happened is conveniently ignored by many commentators on the mystery, which is that one of the ship's lifeboats was missing. This immediately suggests that the ship's company and Captain Briggs' family left the vessel in it. The mystery is why they did so. There may, of course, have been a mutiny, or perhaps some other circumstance prompted them to leave the ship. But it does meant that their loss was not a supernatural disappearance.

Twenty-three years later an iron ship from Liverpool was found floating empty outside Halifax, Nova Scotia. There were signs that those aboard had left the ship in a hurry, although a table had apparently been laid for breakfast. To this day nobody knows what happened to the crew or to the woman passenger (she left behind a chest filled with her clothes) who was sailing with them. Had they abandoned the ship, and if so, why? Or had something or someone removed them from it? The enigma is no nearer being solved today that it was in 1895.

Similarly, in the 1930s, a 75-ton schooner named *Dawn* set sail from Alabama with a cargo of lumber, heading for Barbados. It was commanded by Captain Reg Mitchell, a very experienced seaman who knew the route and the area well, and carried a crew of eight. But despite the weather continuing fair, the ship went missing and failed to arrive at its destination. A look-out was kept for it by Captain Mitchell's fellow skippers and by aircraft flying over the area, but without result. Yet three months later the ship turned up again, being sighted adrift a few miles off the Mexican coast by a solitary fisherman. He notified the coastguards, who went out in a launch to investiate. They found the *Dawn* to be in excellent condition: the sails were neatly furled, the engine was in good running order, and the diesel tanks were more than half full. But of Captain Reg Mitchell and his crew of eight there was no sign. They had disappeared without trace and nobody knows to this day what became of them.

The Caribbean has been the scene of many disappearances as enigmatic as the loss of the crew of the *Dawn*, but none is so mysterious as the vanishing of the ship *Island Queen* and all who were aboard her. Not only does this vessel's disappearance rank as one of the sea's greatest mysteries – one infinitely stranger than the missing crew of the *Mary Celeste* – but the circumstances surrounding its loss perhaps suggest that something more than 'natural causes' was responsible. In fact there is good reason for believing that the *Island Queen* is one of the most likely cases of a marine (and mass) supernatural disappearance.

The drama began on Saturday 5 August 1944, when the 75-ton auxiliary schooner *Island Queen* set sail at 6 p.m. from the port of St George's in Grenada. Aboard the vessel were its crew, consisting of the elderly yet highly capable Captain Salhab and ten seamen, and fifty-seven passengers. The latter were mainly excursionists, who were travelling to the island of St Vincent to take part in the holiday festival there, although some were guests invited to a wedding. The distance between St George's and Kingstown, the port of call, is about seventy-five miles and the voyage should have taken all night, with the boat arriving at its destination at about breakfast the following day. Half an hour after the *Island Queen* commenced sailing, its smaller companion vessel, the *Providence Mark*, also left St George's for Kingstown.

The route of both ships took them along the western side of a chain of islands known as the Grenadines. The *Providence Mark* kept closer to these islands, never getting more than about five miles away from them, yet the *Island Queen* pursued a course further out to sea, sailing by the islands at an estimated distance of between ten and twelve miles. This allowed the *Providence Mark* to catch up and overtake the *Island Queen* at about 9 p.m., when they were off Dusquense. Some reports claim that those aboard the former vessel were able to hear the sounds of singing and guitar playing coming from the *Island Queen*. Certainly the mood aboard the ship would have been light and easy, with everybody enjoying themselves. After all, sailing through a fine Caribbean night can be a magical experience.

The *Providence Mark* continued its course, gradually pulling away from the *Island Queen*, until at about midnight all sight of her was lost in the darkness of the night. The smaller ship then sailed on to reach Kingstown at 9 a.m. on Sunday, where the crew told those waiting that the *Island Queen* was coming along behind and would surely dock before too much time went by. But that supposition was never realized. The whole of Sunday passed without sight of the *Island Queen*. Impatience turned to concern among those on the harbour waiting for friends and relatives, and their concern became anxiety when, at 10.30 p.m., the port officer at Kingstown cabled his opposite number at St George's to ask if the ship had returned there. The reply he received was negative.

The following morning steps were taken to mount a search for the missing ship. Permission was obtained from the owner of the vessel *Rose Marie* for its skipper, Captain Wells, to put to sea in the hope of locating the *Island Queen*. Yet the *Rose Marie*'s departure was delayed because all the crew were on holiday and had to be individually contacted. But a cable was sent to the Royal Naval authorities in Trinidad asking for a search plane. One was speedily dispatched and flew over the area during the afternoon. Nothing, however, was seen by it. The naval authorities at Barbados, St Vincent and St Lucia were contacted and their help was requested. The *Rose Marie* finally set sail at 6.30 p.m. and proceeded south-west towards Grenada. Later, messages were sent to the British Fleet Air Arm and the US Navy department asking for their assistance, and local cargo captains were urged to look out for the missing ship.

The search by sea and air went on for several days without result. At first, hope of the *Island Queen* being found was high, especially as it was known that she carried sufficient food to last, if carefully rationed, for one week. But once this period had expired hope turned to dismay. On 29 August the Governor of the Windward Islands issued a statement which expressed what everybody instinctively felt:

> A close surveillance still continues [he wrote] but it must be realized that in view of the time which has elapsed and the very thorough search which has been conducted, the chance of getting news of the vessel is now remote. It is with sorrow that I am forced to the conclusion that the schooner *Island Queen* must now be presumed lost with all hands.

At no time during the period of the search was anything of the *Island Queen* seen, despite the weather continuing fine. No survivors were picked up. No bodies were discovered afloat nor were any washed ashore. No wreckage was found. No oil patches were sighted on the surface of the sea. The ship had vanished as completely as if she had never been, along with the sixty-eight people aboard. No clue has since been found to suggest what took place on that clear and carefree Caribbean night. It seems likely therefore, if not proven, that the *Island Queen* supernaturally disappeared.

If the supernatural disappearance of a ship sounds totally impossible to the reader, it is pertinent to consider the so-called Philadelphia Experiment which took place in 1943. According to Charles Berlitz and a number of other writers, this mysterious and still secret experiment in invisibility was conducted by the US Navy during the dark days of the Second World War, and which arose from the research being done to produce an electromagnetic defence system capable of protecting ships against incoming torpedoes and other missiles.

Although the details of the Philadelphia Experiment are still uncertain, what broadly happened was this: during the first two weeks of August 1943 a destroyer escort vessel, the USS *Eldridge*, code-numbered DE 173, which had been secretly launched in the June of that year, was berthed at the naval dockyard in Philadelphia, where it and its crew were subjected to enormously powerful pulsating electromagnetic fields generated by motors both aboard the ship and on the dock. The effect of these fields initially created a greenish electrical mist around the USS *Eldridge*, whose structure gradually faded from view within the mist until the whole ship disappeared so completely that only the impression of its hull remained visible in the water.

But optical invisibility was not the only incredible result caused by the pulsating electromagnetic fields, as moments later the hull impression vanished from the water – revealing that the vessel had physically disappeared – and the USS *Eldridge* was then seen by witnesses to suddenly materialize in the dockyard at Norfolk, Virginia, over two hundred miles away! The ship had in other words been teleported there. However, it remained at Norfolk for only two or three minutes, being then returned by the same miraculous method to Philadelphia. But despite the success of the experiment in these regards, it unhappily had very deleterious effects on the crew, many of whom became sick, some mad, while others suffered from the odd effect of becoming invisible when they least expected it, which naturally shocked and frightened those who saw it happen. Two or three men who disappeared in this way never returned, and another two spontaneously caught fire and burned to death. Hence the Philadelphia Experiment, for those participating in it, was a disaster.

Later, sometime in October 1943, the USS *Eldridge* was again subjected to the same high intensity electromagnetic fields, although this time the vessel was anchored well out to sea. Their effects were observed (and filmed) from two other ships, one of which was called the SS *Andrew Fureseth*, and once more a greenish mist enveloped the USS *Eldridge*, within which it soon became invisible. However, this time the vessel was not teleported to another site. Sailors aboard the ship said that although they could still vaguely see each other, the structure of the vessel became completely invisible, so that their comrades appeared to be standing in mid-air rather than upon the decks. Yet the mental and physical effects of the electromagnetic fields upon the crew were as severe as before, with confusion, headaches and loss of balance being among the least unpleasant symptoms. It is believed that these deleterious side-effects were the chief reason why this attempt at making ships invisible was abandoned. It was simply too uncertain and too dangerous.

The Philadelphia Experiment has direct relevance to the subject matter of this book, because if it was a true happening it shows that matter can not only be made optically invisible by high-intensity pulsating electromagnetic fields, but can also be made to disappear by being teleported to a distant site, which is a phenomenon frequently associated with supernatural disappearances. Hence the electromagnetic disappearance and the supernatural disappearance may both be products of the same basic cause. For while high-intensity pulsating electromagnetic fields such as were generated in the Philadelphia Experiment are unlikely to be encountered in nature, it may be that those of lesser intensity arising during thunderstorms, whirlwinds, earthquakes, and solar eclipses, are none the less a contributory factor in some supernatural disappearances.

Aircraft also mysteriously disappear, although less commonly, it must be admitted, than ships. This is probably because most are in continuous radio contact with an airport, which enables any problems to be reported immediately; they frequently fly over land, which allows their wreckage to be more easily spotted in the event of a crash; and they tend to attract larger and more intense searches, doubtlessly because dropping out of the sky is considered by many to be a more tragic and unnatural happening than slipping silently under the waves. Yet as we shall see, there are some aircraft disappearances which are difficult to explain by ordinary means.

The earliest aeroplane loss which may have been a supernatural disappearance is also one of the most touching, involving as it does a curious conspiracy of names and dates. Unlike most aeroplane disappearances, it is distinguished by the fact that it had numerous witnesses.

The disappearance took place immediately before the first New York Times Aerial Derby, an air race flown around the island of Manhattan, which was held on the amazingly inauspicious date of 13 October 1913. This event was ostensibly held to mark the tenth anniversary of the first ever flight by Wilbur Wright in *Kitty Hawk* in 1903, although Wilbur Wright soared aloft on 17 December of that year. The race had sixteen entrants, of whom the thirteenth listed, although he was assigned number 14, was the man who vanished. His name was Albert J. Jewel. This young airman was hoping to win the $1,000 first prize, and he knew that his wife would be delirious with joy if he could bring in his 80 h.p. Bleriot-type Moisan monoplane ahead of the others. After all, they had a 3-year-old daughter and they needed the money.

In 1913 aeroplanes were still a rarity, and the New York Times Aerial Derby naturally attracted a lot of interest from the public. The race was to commence from the Oakwood Heights aerodrome on Staten Island, and as an added spectacle it was arranged that three of the competitors would fly their planes from the Hempstead Plains aerodrome on Long Island across to Oakwood Heights the afternoon before. One of these flyers was to be Albert J. Jewel. 'The aviators will fly, weather permitting,' noted a *New York Times* reporter, 'over Jamaica Bay, Coney Island, and the bay, to the aviation grounds.'

But Albert J. Jewel did not managed to get aloft on that Sunday afternoon. All was not right with his plane's new Nome engine, which he decided needed a little 'tuning up'. So he waved the other two flyers farewell and concentrated on getting the motor into tiptop condition. He had no doubts about his technical ability as he was a trained mechanic. Yet it would have been better had he regarded his unexpected delay as a warning from the gods.

Albert J. Jewel worked on the plane for several hours and went to bed satisfied that he had done a good job. The race was due to start at 3.30 p.m. the following day, which gave him several hours of daylight to fly across to the Oakwood Heights aerodrome. Hardly surprisingly, he slept well and he left his bed in a cheerful mood. After making a detailed final check of his aircraft, the intrepid aviator set off in the Moisan monoplane at about noon and roared aloft into the clear sky. It was the last that anyone would ever see of him.

Albert J. Jewel started to fly from the Hempstead Plains aviation field ... but he did not reach his destination [reported the *New York Times*]. So far as could be learned no one knew what became of him after he disappeared from view of those watching him leave Hempstead Plains sailing rapidly southwest, and it is feared by many that he had met with a serious mishap ... he has been lost as completely *as if he had evaporated into air* [author's italics]. His death by drowning in Jamaica Bay or far out to sea is greatly feared, as it is said he cannot swim.

The reporter's comments about the completeness of Albert J. Jewel's disappearance were not exaggerated. A search for him and his plane was quickly organized, both on land and at sea. The Jamaica Bay marshes, Coney Island, Rockaway, Far Rockaway and other places were either visited or reached by telephone. Volunteers in boats put to sea. But their efforts were entirely without result. Neither Albert J. Jewel's body nor any remains of his aeroplane were ever found. Both man and machine had vanished without trace. Yet when competitor William Walb lost control of his aircraft later that afternoon and came down in the narrows of the bay, he was picked up by the Quarantine station steamboat within five minutes.

For the first New York Times Aerial Derby did go ahead, even though only five of the competitors managed to get airborne from the Staten Island airfield. The winner, entrant number 7, set off in his 100 h.p. Curtiss biplane at 3.33 p.m. and flew around Manhattan to cross the winning line in the remarkably speedy time of 54 minutes and 55 seconds. His name, believe it or not, was W.S. Luckey!

Since that time many aeroplanes have mysteriously disappeared. I say 'mysteriously' meaning that the cause of their loss and the whereabouts of the aircraft, crew and any passengers are unknown. Some of these disappearances may have been supernatural, although there are of course a number of other ways to account for them, which range from sudden and unexpected equipment malfunction right across the spectrum of possibility to abduction by UFOs. No aeroplane to my knowledge has vanished while being watched by reputable witnesses, which is the main criterion for a disappearance being classified as supernatural, yet many have done so while being monitored electronically, by radio, by radar, or by both. When such a disappearance happens suddenly in good weather conditions, and if the subsequent search turns up no wreckage at all, then it may quite reasonably be postulated that the aircraft and those aboard have supernaturally disappeared.

The most famous happening said to be of this type involved not one but five planes, all TBM Avenger torpedo bombers, known as Flight 19, which flew east from Fort Lauderdale, Florida, on 5 December 1945, and vanished over that part of the Atlantic ocean now referred to as the Bermuda Triangle. The planes and their crews were on a training exercise.

Most of the fourteen crewmen were students, only two being experienced officers. Yet instead of the scheduled two-hour outing they should have had, Flight 19 was evidently unable to find its way back to its base, which accounted for the five hours the Avengers spent in the air before they disappeared. The loss is made more puzzling by the fact that Flight 19's leader, Lt Charles Taylor, was disorientated by the failure of both of his plane's compasses, that radio communication between the flyers and their base was strangely intermittent, and that the extensive five-day search for the planes failed to locate any wreckage, life-rafts or bodies.

The disappearance of Flight 19 has been extensively written about and all manner of weird and wonderful reasons have been given to account for it. I won't try the reader's patience by discussing them. However, it seems to me that because the TBM Avenger torpedo bomber could only fly for five hours, it is likely that the planes, by running out of fuel, were forced to come down in the sea. They then presumably sank rapidly. But because the crash site was not precisely known, it was either missed completely by the searchers or the wreckage was dispersed by the elements beforehand and so overlooked. The real mystery of Flight 19, therefore, is not the planes vanishing, but the circumstances leading up to it.

However, two other aircraft disappearances which took place not long afterwards are sufficiently puzzling to perhaps qualify as 'supernatural'. The first happened in 1948, the year after the loss of Flight 19, and the second in 1949. Both involved the same airline and the same type of aeroplane, yet whereas one went missing within the Bermuda Triangle, the other was lost well outside it.

On Thursday 29 January 1948, a British South American Airways Tudor IV airliner named *Star Tiger* set off from the Azores to fly to Bermuda. This was the last leg of a flight which had begun in London, touched down first at Lisbon, and then gone on to the Azores. Aboard were a crew of six, led by Captain D. Colby, and twenty-five passengers, who included the well-known Second World War air commander Air Marshal Sir Arthur Coningham. The plane was due to land at Bermuda at six o'clock on Friday morning, 30 January.

At 11.15 p.m. a routine message was received from Radio Officer R. Tuck aboard the *Star Tiger*, giving her position as 440 miles north-east of Bermuda. In the event it proved to be her last communication, for nothing was ever heard from or of the plane again. No distress signals were sent, and there was no suggestion of any trouble within or outside the plane during that last message.

The loss of radio contact alerted the authorities to the fact that something untoward had happened and a search was quickly mounted, the first plane leaving Bermuda at 3.15 a.m. Friday 30 January. The search was large and carefully coordinated, involving as it did United States military aircraft as well as civilian aircraft flying out from Bermuda, backed up by search and rescue units operating from Newfoundland and from bases sited along the eastern seaboard of the United States. It was scheduled to continue until any wreckage or survivors were found, yet even after fifteen hours of concentrated looking no trace of either was seen. Despite several days of further effort nothing from the plane was located. Indeed, the *Star Tiger* and all aboard her had completely and inexplicably vanished.

Following the loss of *Star Tiger* all Tudor IV aircraft were grounded and subjected to reliability trials, which prevented them from returning to the Bermuda run for eleven weeks. The Ministry of Civil Aviation also appointed a court of investigation to examine *Star Tiger*'s disappearance, but it turned up nothing that could in any way explain what had taken place. The report concluded: 'What happened will never be known and the aircraft's fate must remain an unsolved mystery.'

Yet tragically and equally mysteriously a second British South American Airways Tudor IV airliner was lost almost exactly one year later. Named *Star Ariel*, it was a sister aircraft to the *Star Tiger*. It commenced its scheduled flight in London and flew to Bermuda, although its final destination was Santiago, Chile. *Star Ariel* left Bermuda on Monday 17 January 1949 at 8 a.m. local time, heading for Kingston, Jamaica. Aboard were Captain J.C. McPhee and a crew of six, and thirteen passengers. It was during that five-and-a-half-hour flight that the plane vanished without trace.

At 8.42 a.m. the *Star Ariel* radioed a routine message giving its position as 150 miles south-west of Bermuda and its height as 18,000 feet. The weather conditions were reported to be good. But as with the *Star Tiger*, it was the last message received. Further radio contact with the plane was lost, and an air rescue aircraft was soon dispatched from Bermuda to search for it. When this found nothing a major rescue operation was begun, which involved twelve United States Navy and coastguard aircraft and eight from Bermuda, as well as other planes, and which continued for several days. In fact it was not until 22 January 1949, that the hunt for the missing airliner was called off. *The Times* of 23 January reported: 'After completing flights totalling more than a million miles aircraft from Kindley, the United States Air Force Base at Bermuda, last night gave up the search for the missing British South American Airways machine *Star Ariel*.'

The losses of the *Star Ariel* and of the *Star Tiger* were virtually identical. The radio officers of both aircraft broadcast routine messages giving information about their plane's position and height, and reported that the weather was good. There was no hint of any problems. Then radio contact was lost and the planes did not arrive at their destinations. Extensive searches for both aircraft failed to find any wreckage whatsoever, and nothing is known to this day of what became of either. The planes' disappearance was sudden, unexpected and total. Like the vessel *Island Queen*, they vanished as completely as if they had never been. And this perhaps suggests that they supernaturally disappeared.

11   The Medium is the Message

On her knees she laid the infant,
On her lap she laid the infant,
And began to brush his hair straight,
And began to smooth his hair down,
When from off her knees he vanished,
From her lap the infant vanished.
　　Marjatta the hapless maiden
Fell into the greatest trouble,
And she hurried off to seek him ...

From Runo 50 of the *Kalevala*

A strange disappearance, involving not one child, as portrayed in
the quote from the *Kalevala* above, but three, took place in the
year 1906. It was recorded by author Harold T. Wilkins, one of the
many people who helped search for them, in his book *Mysteries:
Solved and Unsolved*. Fortunately, however, the missing children
were not lost for ever.

According to Wilkins, in June 1906 the three children of a
railway brakeman named Vaughan – his son aged ten, and his two
daughters, aged three and five – went to play in a large pasture
field known as Forty Acres, which lay near to a Midland Railway
locomotive engine-shed about one mile outside the city of
Gloucester. They had often played in the field before and their
parents had no reason to think that they would come to any harm.
But the children did not return home for their tea, and when Mr
and Mrs Vaughan went to look for them they were alarmed to
discover that they could not find them. The police were therefore
contacted, and a large search party consisting of policemen and
volunteers was soon organized.

For three days and nights [says Wilkins], scores of people, including the cleaners from the locomotive shed, searched every inch of the 'Forty Acres'. We paid particular attention to the north-east corner of the field, where the pasture was bordered by tall, old elms, a thick hedge of thorn and bramble, and a deep ditch, separating it from a corn-field. Every inch was probed with sticks, and not a stone was left unturned in the ditch. Had a dead dog been dumped there, he would certainly have been found. Not a trace of the missing children was found.

The police had absolutely no idea what had become of the children, although it was soon obvious that they had not lost themselves anywhere in the locality, as otherwise they would have been found. So after three fruitless days without finding either of them or any clue to their whereabouts, there seemed little point in continuing the search. The missing children, it was decided, had either left, or had been taken from, the area, and might therefore never be seen alive again.

But then, much to everybody's amazement, at 6 a.m. on the fourth day, a farm worker walking to work along the edge of the corn-field abutting Forty Acres happened to look over the hedge standing between the two fields – and to his surprise saw the three Vaughan children lying asleep in the ditch! The children were none the worse for wear and they were not particularly hungry, but they were startled to learn that people had been out looking for them. All they could remember, they said, was going to sleep in the ditch. Indeed, when the Vaughan son was interviewed forty years later about the mystery, he stated that 'he had not the slightest recollection, nor ever had had, of what had happened between the time when he and his sisters were missing in the Forty Acre field, and when he and they were found, asleep in the ditch'.

But how could three young children survive for three days out of doors, without food, without becoming famished, very dirty and unkempt, and very distressed? And where could they have been to remain hidden from scores of searchers? There are only two possible solutions: either they were taken in by an adult and cared for during the three days or they supernaturally vanished on the day they went missing and were only returned to that well-searched ditch at or near the start of the fourth day.

The first of these two alternatives might seem the most likely, although it is hard to imagine how an adult could have tempted the children into his or her home and then kept them there without the neighbours noticing them, or hearing them, for three days. If they had been hidden in this way, it would surely have been revealed by the children, if not immediately then sometime later in their lives. But none of them ever admitted it. All in fact said that they had no memory of what had happened to them. They went, as it were, straight from being in the Forty Acres to being asleep in the ditch. The three days were seemingly lost to them, just as they became lost to the world during those three days.

It is possible, therefore, that the Vaughan children were temporarily removed from our dimension and taken into another, whose time, like that of the fairy world, passes far more slowly than here, with the result that a few minutes spent there equalled the passing of three days in our world. If the children had lost consciousness on entry into that dimension, they would have no awareness, and hence no memory, of it at all. On their return they were deposited asleep in the Forty Acres' ditch, blissfully ignorant of what had happened to them or of the search that had been conducted for them. Hence their surprise when they discovered the alarm that their 'few minutes' of innocent sleep had caused!

However, such time dislocation is rare; it is far commoner, as we have seen, for someone to supernaturally vanish at one place and then immediately reappear somewhere else, which might be some distance away. It is also rare for two or more people to disappear together and then to simultaneously reappear.

Teleportation, like the out-of-body experience, is essentially a 'one-off' event. It happens when the conditions are somehow uniquely right for it to do so, but it is seldom repeated. And because it occurs without warning, it is very difficult for the subject to be at all prepared for it. This is why the process itself is so little understood and why it seems scarcely credible.

Yet teleportation is one of the many marvels that may happen to the best spiritualist mediums; and it is certainly the most highly regarded 'physical' phenomenon.

At least two well-known nineteenth-century mediums supernaturally disappeared from one spot and spontaneously, and instantly, materialized at another. This was most remarkable in the case of the first, Mrs Samuel Guppy, who on 3 June 1871, while ensconced in her Highbury sitting-room with her companion

Miss Neyland, clad only in a loose dressing-gown and slippers, suddenly vanished from Miss Neyland's presence to materialize with a scream and a loud bump on a table three miles away at 61 Lamb's Conduit Street, WC1, around which a seance was in progress. Her sudden teleportation there had resulted, it was said, from one of the sitters (of whom there were ten) jokingly asking the spirit control to bring the obese, 17-stone Mrs Guppy into the room. The spirit was evidently able to oblige without difficulty!

William Eglinton was another famous materialization medium of the period, but even he was surprised by his teleportation from a seance held at 21 Green Street, Grosvenor Square, W1, on the evening of 16 March 1878. The seance took place around a table in a darkened first floor room, and the participants included two other mediums, namely Arthur Colman and J.W. Fletcher, and four ordinary sitters, two of whom were women. The shutters of the room and its door were closed and locked, and they would have admitted revealing light if they had been opened at any time during the spiritualist session.

The teleportation of William Eglinton likewise occurred, interestingly enough, when one of the sitters, W.H. Harrison, 'half seriously asked if the spirits could take Mr Colman through the ceiling by way of giving a variety of manifestation'. It was then remarked by two of the sitters, who would have been holding his hands, that Eglinton had left the circle, and immediately a loud bump was heard overhead, as if the man himself had suddenly been deposited on the floor upstairs. Someone immediately lit the light.

> When the light was struck, Mr Eglinton was not in the room. Mr George Sutherland unlocked the door by turning the key which was in the lock ... Mrs Gregory and several sitters proceeded upstairs, and found Mr Eglinton lying in a deep trance on the floor with his arms extended. This was about two minutes after he disjoined hands in the room below. In two or three minutes he revived and complained of the back of his head being hurt, as if by a blow; beyond this there was nothing the matter with him and he was as well as before in a few minutes.

An even more remarkable teleportation is reported of the famous South American medium Carlo Mirabelli, whose capacity for producing dramatic physical phenomena – apports, telekinesis, levitation, etc. – in daylight before reputable witnesses made him one of the most talented and exceptional mediums that have ever lived.

Mirabelli was born in 1889 at Botucatu in the state of Sao Paulo, Brazil (he died in 1951), and it was from the Est da Luz railway station at the state capital of Sao Paulo, in 1926, that his miraculous disappearance occurred. He had gone to the station with a group of friends to catch a train to the port of Santos. The train was at the platform and some of the party were climbing aboard, when Mirabelli, who had stepped a few paces away from them to bid farewell to a friend who was not travelling with him, suddenly began to physically fade away. This brought cries of alarm and wonder from the friend and from those who happened to catch sight of the startling event, which naturally directed the attention of everyone nearby to what was happening, for Mirabelli continued to vanish into a smoke-like haze until he and his clothes and personal effects were literally no longer there. He had completely disappeared, in broad daylight and in front of dozens of witnesses, on a railway platform.

Those whom Mirabelli left behind were not only astonished, but were also very worried and perplexed, as they had not the slightest idea what had become of him. Yet their anxieties were fortunately soon put to rest, although their wonder grew, when fifteen minutes later the station master received a telephone call from the medium, who revealed that he had materialized in, and was speaking from, the town of Sao Vincente, which stood near to Santos on the coast and about ninety kilometres or fifty-six miles away from Sao Paulo! But the journey there had not taken him that long; in fact it must have been instantaneous, as by the time he had materialized there, taken in what had occurred, realized that he was in another place, spoken to a person whom he recognized, who witnessed his arrival, and glanced at his watch, only two minutes had gone by. It was to take several more minutes of joyfully coming to terms with what had happened, and of adjusting to the fact that he was in a town so far away, before Mirabelli thought to telephone the railway station at Est da Luz and tell his friends, whom he realized would be worried sick about him, that he was safe and well, but at a considerable distance from them.

The teleportation of Carlo Mirabelli was a sudden, spontaneous affair, which does not seem to have been brought on by any particular need or wish on his part to go to Sao Vincente. He also experienced no amnesia or mental confusion when he materialized, but quickly adjusted to what had happened, presumably because he was somewhat used to dealing with such strange and remarkable events.

A couple of years later, Mirabelli underwent another, although by comparison far more modest, teleportation: in a near repetition of William Eglinton's vanishing, he supernaturally disappeared from a locked seance room, wherein he was also tied to his chair, and from the presence of five sitters, and was later found, reclining in an armchair and singing a popular song, in an adjacent room!

One medium who vanished from a seance room was seemingly as unlikely a subject for the role he was playing as was the fact of his teleportation. For he was none other than the Marquis Carlo Centurione Scotto, a distinguished Italian aristocrat, whose interest in contacting the spirits of the dead was only aroused, and whose ability to do so was only discovered, following the tragic death of his eldest son Vittorio in a flying accident in 1926. Indeed, the Marquis exercised his mediumistic powers, which were considerable, for a period of about two years, after which he ceased to communicate any further with those who had died.

The seance to which I refer took place at the Marquis's magnificent summer residence and ancestral home, Millesimo Castle, situated in north-western Italy, on 29 July 1928. An account of the happenings on that night, written by one of the participants, the eminent psychic researcher Professor Ernesto Bozzano, was published in the September–October 1928 edition of the magazine *Luce e Ombre* (Light and Dark). The nine other individuals making up the circle included the Marquis's wife, Luisa Centurione Scotto, M. and Mme Rossi, Mrs Gwendolyn Hack, and lawyer M. Piero Bon. Mme Rossi and Mrs Hack were also mediums, but with different abilities to those of the Marquis. They were in fact all educated adults, and presumably not easily duped.

Most of the seance, which was held in darkness in a downstairs room of Millesimo Castle, was taken up by a long conversation between the Marquis's spirit guide, named Cristo d'Angelo, and M. Piero Bon, after which, 'at the end of the sitting,' Professor Bozzano tells us, 'we had an extraordinary phenomenon, one of the rarest in the annals of metapsychical research, which caused us all the most terrible anxiety for two and a half hours.'

This 'extraordinary phenomenon' was the disappearance of Marquis Centurione Scotto. His vanishing was preceded by some other unusual phenomena, which included icy blasts of air, the movement of a heavy table, and several muffled raps from different parts of the room. Following the latter, M. Rossi twice thought he heard the medium move from his chair, although on calling out to him, Marquis Centurione Scotto was able to assure him of his continued presence. What happened next was equally dramatic: 'Suddenly he exclaimed in a frightened voice: "I can no longer feel my legs!" At that moment the gramophone stopped, and in the general anxiety caused by the medium's exclamation, no one thought of restarting it. An interval of death-like silence followed.'

The Marquise Centurione Scotto, becoming frightened, next called out loudly to her husband but received no reply. Another sitter, M. Castellani, was similarly disappointed. An attempt to detect the Marquis by touch revealed that both his chair and a nearby sofa were empty. Professor Bozzano then opined that the Marquis had probably been teleported or, as he calls it, 'asported' from the room. To determine if this was so, a red light was switched on, which showed that he was in fact no longer present, despite the door still being locked from the inside.

Professor Bozzano continues:

> We searched for him in adjacent rooms, but found no one ... At this moment a terrible anxiety tormented us all. With great caution M. Castellani and M. Passini searched all the rooms of the castle, but their return only increased our alarm, for they found no one, absolutely no one ... Meanwhile two and a half hours had passed in our vain search of the castle. The cellars, the stables, the family chapel, and even the grounds had been explored.

A successful attempt was next made to locate the Marquis by calling on the spirits for help. This was done by Mrs Hack, an automatist, who was told that her host was sleeping in one of the castle's outbuildings: 'Go to the right, then outside. Wall and Gate. He is lying – hay – hay – in a soft place.' These directions led to a fresh search of the stables, where snores were heard emerging from behind a small door that had previously been overlooked.

This door was locked, the key being in the keyhole on the outside of the door. We opened it with great caution, and we immediately saw two well-shod feet pointing towards the door ... On a heap of hay and oats the medium was comfortably lying, immersed in a profound sleep. M. Castellani made a few magnetic passes over the Marquis, and almost immediately he commenced to move, groaning pitifully. When he first began to regain consciousness and found himself lying in the stable on the hay and oats, with M. Passini and M. Castellani near him, he completely lost his bearings, feared that he had gone out of his mind and burst into tears.

If the teleportation of the Marquis Centurione Scotto was genuine, as it appears to have been, it is no wonder that he was overcome when he woke from his trance-like sleep. The shock to his nervous system would have been considerable, although fortunately he did not suffer any long-term ill-effects.

And while the Marquis's sudden and unwished-for translocation to a stable was comparatively short in distance (about one hundred yards in total), his removal there remains one of the most compelling examples of this remarkable phenomenon, even though his apparent supernatural disappearance from a darkened room cannot be as persuasive to the sceptic as the daylight vanishing of Carlo Mirabelli.

But while desire seemingly played no part in the Marquis Centurione Scotto's 'asportation', it was certainly a factor in the fortunate and timely movement made by W. Tudor Pole, which he described under the heading 'Transit Most Mysterious' in his book *The Silent Road*.

Pole says that one evening in December 1952, when he was expecting an important long-distance telephone call at his Sussex home, the train bringing him from London arrived late at the local station, which lay one and a half miles away from where he lived. Frustratingly, it was pouring with rain, the bus had gone, there were no taxis, and the station telephone was out of service! He went into the waiting-room in near despair, thinking that he must certainly miss his 6 p.m. call, the time then being 5.57 p.m.

What happened next I cannot say [he writes]. When I came to myself I was standing in my hall at home, a good twenty minutes' walk away, and the clock was striking six. My telephone call duly came through a few minutes later ... Having finished my call, I awoke to the realization that something very strange had happened. Then much to my surprise, I found that my shoes were dry and free from mud, and that my clothes showed no sign of damp or damage.

If Pole has accurately represented the time he was in the waiting-room – and we have, it must be admitted, only his word for it – then it would have been impossible for him even to have sprinted home by six o'clock. A journey on foot would also have soaked him through to the skin. It is even doubtful if he could have got back by six o'clock had a friend suddenly turned up and given him a lift. Not only would his friend have found it difficult to drive sufficiently fast along the narrow country lanes in the dark with the rain pouring down, but the time remaining would have been partly taken up by his meeting with that person, by his requesting a lift and explaining his need to get home, and then by the dash from the waiting-room to the car and from the car in to his house. The latter would likewise have exposed him to the rain.

This suggests that, unless Pole lied or was hopelessly befuddled on the day in question, the only way he could have reached his house in time to take the call was to be supernaturally shifted there by teleportation, which means that he would have vanished from the railway station waiting-room and instantly rematerialized in his own home. That is what he seems to have believed happened to him, although he does not speculate as to how it came about.

However, it must be admitted that there are many cases on record of people who have suddenly, for one reason or another, lost their memories, so that they both forget who they are and where they live, and who wander off, sometimes to travel hundreds or even thousands of miles before their memory returns, although they cannot remember how they got where they are. These cases, perhaps not surprisingly, are sometimes mistakenly referred to as examples of teleportation.

The most famous of such false teleportees was a 21-year-old South African man named Thomas R. Kessel, who was found wandering the streets of New York in a confused state on 3 May 1956. He did not know where he was or how he had got there. He was taken to Bellevue Hospital, where it was discovered that the last thing he could remember was sitting in a bar in Johannesburg on 10 April, drinking with some friends. After that everything was a complete blank.

The mystery deepened when it was found that he had no documentation with him. How then had he arrived in the United States? Was it by a miraculous teleportation, reminiscent of that made by Gil Perez, or had his journey there been far more ordinary? There were some who thought that the former possibility was the answer, although the length of time between 10 April and 3 May – a little over three weeks – suggested that the latter was far more likely.

And so it turned out to be. Enquiries made by the authorities determined that Kessel had crossed the Atlantic as a deck-hand on the Danish cargo ship *Nordhval*. The ship had first docked at Mobile, in Alabama, where Kessel, while darning a hole in one of his socks, had unfortunately coughed and thereby swallowed the other needle he was holding in his mouth. He was rushed to hospital to have the needle removed from his throat, which resulted in him missing the departure of the *Nordhval* for its next port of call, New York.

On his release from hospital, the operation having been a success, Kessel made his way to New York, but found that the *Nordhval* had already left without him. He therefore went to the Danish Consul, from whom he collected his wages, which had been deposited with them. It was then that he unaccountably lost his memory (and his passport), and the mental confusion this caused led to him being taken into the Bellevue Hospital. But after six days of psychiatric treatment, Kessel fully regained his memory and it wasn't long before the Cape Town-based shipping firm who had employed him paid for his return to South Africa. And so the mystery was solved!

But much genuine mystery still surrounds the powers of Uri Geller, whose abilities as a psychic metal-bender have amazed, delighted, and even disturbed millions. Less well-known is his tendency to cause the materialization and dematerialization of inanimate objects in his vicinity, like vases, ashtrays and keys, and on one famous occasion he may have been unwittingly responsible for the transportation of a dog.

The latter event took place while he was staying with Dr Adrija Puharich, the celebrated parapsychological researcher, in early November 1972. This is how Geller describes what happened in his autobiography *My Story*:

The day after we arrived in Ossining, I noticed Andrija's black retriever, Wellington, lying in the kitchen doorway and trembling noticeably. The telephone rang, and Andrija went to answer it in the kitchen. It was in my mind that he would have to step over the dog, but suddenly Wellington just wasn't there. I don't mean he got up and ran away. He was there one second and not there the next, just like some of the inanimate things that had been appearing and disappearing.

Within seconds, I saw the dog far down the driveway and coming towards the house. We called to him, and he came, still trembling and upset. We were all shocked. No one could make any sense of it. As Andrija said, how could a living thing be translocated like this in a matter of seconds?

It would be interesting of course to know why Wellington was trembling before he vanished. Something had obviously frightened the dog, but what? Was it an ordinary happening in or around the house which had just spooked him? – or had he sensed that some force or energy, which may have originated from Geller, was taking him over? If the first is right, then we have an example of how even a dog can be teleported by its own fear, while if the second is true, the force involved, from wherever it comes, may be the causative agent of many human translocations.

Uri Geller's witnessing of Wellington's supernatural disappearance from the kitchen doorway and the dog's materialization at the bottom of the driveway strangely foreboded his own teleportation almost exactly one year later. And although Geller vanished while jogging along a street in New York, he materialized again just outside Puharich's house in Ossining, about thirty-three miles away. Wellington, however, was in no way disconcerted by Geller's sudden crashing entry, as apparently he did not even bark!

This is what happened: on the afternoon of Friday 9 November 1973, shortly after 6 p.m., Geller left a store called Hammacher–Schlemmer's in Manhattan, where he had gone to buy a present for his date of that evening, and jogged back towards his apartment, where he intended to shower and change before meeting the woman at 6.30 p.m. He did not have far to go, and only two or three minutes later he recalled reaching the apartment building standing next to his own. What happened next, which it did without any warning, was startling:

I remember having the feeling that I was running backwards for a couple of steps. I don't know whether I really did or not, but that was the feeling. Then I had the feeling that I was being sucked upwards. There was no sensation in my body. I closed my eyes and, I think, opened them almost immediately.

The fleeting glimpse Geller had of his surroundings showed him that he was no longer in Manhattan. He was no longer jogging either, but falling out of the air. He next struck a light porch screen, tore through it, and collided with the glass-topped wooden table below, knocking it over and smashing the glass, before striking the floor, where he lay shocked and bruised, and wondering if he had broken any bones. He was still clutching the pair of binoculars he had bought earlier. It did not take him long to recognize where he was: he had fallen into the porch of Andrija Puharich's house at Ossining!

The noise of Geller's sudden entry and his subsequent shouts soon brought Puharich, who at first thought that a tree had fallen on the porch, to the scene. Though surprised, he quickly checked Geller out and determined that he was uninjured. Puharich was able to report that he had heard the crash Geller made half-way through the TV news broadcast he was watching, at about 6.15 p.m. The telephone then rang, the caller proving to be Maria Janis, a Manhattan-dwelling friend of Geller's with whom he had been until 5.30 p.m. She knew that Geller couldn't possibly have reached Puharich's house by any ordinary means in forty-five minutes. Yet Geller's translocation to Ossining had been far swifter, having taken virtually no time at all.

This led the astonished Uri Geller to ask: 'What kind of transformation or transportation did my body undergo? Was I really torn up molecule by molecule? Was I pushed through a dimension, teleported by a ray or by a spacecraft? What happened? I don't know.'

And with that puzzled cry I must bring this long catalogue of supernatural disappearances to an end. We have examined many of the most celebrated cases of this startling, enigmatic and wonderful phenomenon, and also many that are little known. You will not, I think, be unimpressed by the sheer number of such seemingly impossible events, which may perhaps convince you that what you thought you understood about the world needs some modification.

It is almost as if we are confined in a prison whose walls are at one and the same time more impenetrable than the strongest steel, for we cannot by any means force ourselves out from this dimension of being, and yet also, when the conditions are somehow right for a passage through them, as unresistant to material penetration as the surface of a soap bubble.

We find a resonance of this in the *Tao Te Ching*, which states: 'The most submissive thing in the world can ride roughshod over the hardest in the world – that which is without substance entering that which has no crevices.'

12 Comments and Conclusions

The Queen had had melancholy forebodings of late, founded
upon an ancient Prophecy, laid up in the records of Fairy
Land, that the date of Fairy existence should be then extinct,
when men should cease to believe in them. And she knew
how the race of the Nymphs, which were her predecessors,
and had been the Guardians of the sacred floods, and of the
silver mountains, had utterly disappeared before the chilling
touch of man's incredulity.

From *The Defeat of Time* by Elia

During this survey of supernatural disappearances and appearances we have travelled far both in distance and time, and we have
examined numerous odd and scarcely believable case histories. I
have done my best to bring you the facts of each case, and where
alternative accounts exist I have given them. But while many are
attested to by witnesses, it must be admitted that such witnesses
may be mistaken in what they said they saw, or they may
exaggerate or even lie. Hence I do not claim that every case I have
presented can necessarily be taken at face value, although together
their very number and surprising similarity suggest that most are
genuine supernatural events. Yet if only one is true it would still
present us with a great mystery, which would seemingly contradict
all that our everyday experience tells us about the working of the
world.

However, before an attempt is made to explain what might be
happening, it will help to list the principal types of supernatural
departures and arrivals. These are:

1) The spontaneous total disappearance, whereby a person,
animal or object vanishes, never to be seen again. About one

fifth of the cases I have discussed are of this type.

2) The spontaneous disappearance of a living person or animal followed by their instantaneous or near instantaneous appearance somewhere else. This is the commonest scenario, happening in about one third of the cases I have examined.

3) The willed disappearance of a person followed by his or her instantaneous or near instantaneous reappearance at a nearby or distant spot. About twelve per cent of the cases I have considered reveal some desire on either the part of the person concerned or of those with him or her at the time.

4) The total disappearance of a dead person. This is a very rare happening.

5) The disappearance of a dead person followed by the corpse's reappearance elsewhere. This is likewise very rare.

6) The disappearance of a dead person followed by his or her reappearance elsewhere, but alive. This too is very rare.

7) The spontaneous appearance which is not preceded, as far as is known, by a disappearance elsewhere. About twelve per cent of the cases I have considered are of this type.

8) The appearance of a double or duplicate, which, because it originates from someone in a trance state, may be considered as willed. The double is conscious and can communicate with those around it. It usually appears some distance away from its source.

9) The spontaneous appearance of a double from a conscious, though possibly distressed, person. It usually appears close to its source although it can on occasions appear far away. Such duplication typically happens only once, if at all, in a person's lifetime, but may occur more frequently.

It is also helpful to reiterate the factors accompanying some of the supernatural disappearances I have mentioned, which may have played a part in bringing them about. These seem to apply only to the spontaneous disappearances of people, not to those of animals or objects.

1) A heightened emotional state caused by frustrated love, anxiety for the welfare of a loved one or others, the fear of being morally compromised, etc.

2) The intense stress caused by a fear of death or other terrors, or by actual death.

3) A strong wish or desire to be elsewhere.

4) A violent thunderstorm.

5) A solar eclipse.

6) Beautiful 'fairy' music or birdsong.

Of these factors, the first three are internal or psychological, the last three are external or physical.

However, while a violent thunderstorm and a solar eclipse are both external, physical factors, both could poduce abject terror in nervous or sensitive individuals, which might therefore be the real cause of an accompanying supernatural disappearance. Yet it is also possible that the electromagnetic disturbances caused by thunderstorms and eclipses are the prime factor, although if so it is hard to understand why, when such a disappearance happens, only one person should vanish and not others nearby. This might perhaps be explained by supposing that the type of terror brought on by an eclipse or a thunderstorm, which is only experienced by certain people, has to be allied with the electromagnetic disturbances also created by them before such a disappearance can occur. Hence a unique combination of natural factors may really be responsible for the supernatural event.

Regarding the beautiful music or birdsong that precedes some supernatural disappearances, it is fascinating to note that legend does give certain music a remarkable power. The singing and lyre playing of Orpheus, for example, not only charmed wild animals but caused trees and rocks to move. It may therefore be that music or birdsong originating from another realm has the power to dematerialize matter in this one.

But none the less, it is very hard to determine what caused or brought about most of the disappearances I have examined which were not accompanied or preceded by any of the factors I have listed above. Indeed, it or they are as much a mystery as the event itself.

However, it is important to ask how something as seemingly impossible as the supernatural disappearance squares with what we know about physics.

You, the book you are holding, and the chair upon which you sit, are material objects. You and they also happen to be solid in nature, although the density of your different body parts varies quite considerably, as it also does, although to a lesser extent, beween the various components of your book and your chair. For example, your skeleton is the densest and most rigid part of you, whereas your fat and muscles are softer and much more flexible. Some portions of you, like your blood, saliva and lymph, are not solid at all, but liquid. Indeed, the chemical compound making up most of your volume (about 70%) is water, which is formed from the combination of two gases, hydrogen and oxygen. Hence in this regard alone your solidity is largely illusory.

But solidity of any kind proves to be a mirage when the building blocks of matter, the atoms, are examined. Instead of the minute solid balls they were once thought to be, atoms are now known to be composed of even smaller, or subatomic, particles, two types of which, the protons and neutrons, form each atom's tiny central nucleus, around which a third and much smaller type of particle, the electron, revolves, the whole having a structure something like a miniature solar system. In fact the electrons are as distant from the atomic nucleus, in proportion to their size, as the major planets are from the sun.

This brief description of atomic structure should make it immediately clear that every atom consists almost entirely of empty space. Some figures should help you understand how empty an atom really is. If we compare, for instance, the volume of an atom to that of its nucleus (where most of its mass is concentrated), the proportions of each are in the region of 10,000,000,000,000 to 1 – that is, ten trillion to one! This enormous preponderance of empty space over mass in a single atom applies equally to the whole of your body and mine. Hence if every atom of our bodies not only collapsed inwards but also nudged up to their neighbours, thereby removing empty space from the equation, our size would diminish to the extent that we would become completely invisible, not just to the naked eye but to even the most powerful of microscopes. Indeed, we would all become so small that the entire human population of the world, thus contracted, could be comfortably placed on the full stop at the end of this sentence. (Our weights, however, would remain the same, so this would result in an enormously heavy full stop!)

But more confusingly, the protons and neutrons of the atomic nucleus are now known to have their own internal structure, both particle types consisting of three even smaller or sub-subatomic particle called quarks. But electrons and quarks are not simply ultra-minute pieces of matter, for although they behave, in certain situations, like particles, in others they act as waves, as indeed does light itself. They are in fact, like the photons of light, quanta of energy, whose 'solidity' derives wholly from the forces they produce, these being 1) electromagnetism, 2) gravity, 3) the weak force, and 4) the strong force, rather than being a property of themselves.

This means that if these forces holding together the subatomic particles and the atoms of our bodies could be somehow negated, then we would vanish into nothing in an instant. This would, of course, be a form of disappearance, although 'dissolution' is a better word to describe what would happen. As we have noted, some people have reportedly vanished 'like a puff of smoke', which may mean that they suffered this end. However, if such total disintegration can happen, it is anybody's guess what circumstances or conditions bring it about.

But although we are little more than packages of empty space made seemingly solid by atomic forces, we have one, possibly two, additional components which distinguish us from the rocks beneath our feet and the air that we breath. The first is our mind, and the second, although some would dispute its existence, is our soul. Neither is physical, which means they are infinitely more 'empty' than the near nothingness of our bodies. Yet they are 'us' – you and me – in a far more intimate sense than are our bodies, and they may, perhaps in a united form, survive the death of our physical selves. In this respect they offer us the hope of immortality and of ultimate freedom.

Because the mind and the soul contain the knowledge of who we are, and because the separated mind/soul can instantly travel to anywhere it wishes, the secret of understanding supernatural disappearances and the often associated teleportation of the physical body probably therefore lies with them. It may be, for example, that the mind/soul combination can, in certain rare situations, reduce us instantly to a sub-microscopic particle of vibrating energy, and then project us, by thought alone, to a distant point at light speed, where it then spatially inflates us in the blink of an eye. We would thus vanish in one place and reappear instantaneously in another.

We have become familiar with the idea of teleportation from science fiction TV shows like *Star Trek*, and we know that it may actually have been accomplished during the 1943 Philadelphia Experiment. During the latter, if I may remind you, a ship and its crew were subjected to extremely powerful high intensity electromagnetic waves, which were able, if the reports are true, to make them both invisible and to teleport them to a distant place, if only temporarily. But neither *Star Trek* nor the Philadelphia Experiment helps to explain how a ship and other non-living objects, or even a herd of cattle, can be spontaneously teleported from one place to another. In fact teleportation seems even less believable than an outright supernatural disappearance.

But such instantaneous movements are contemplated with equanimity by physicists discussing the properties of black holes, which are super-dense stellar objects formed from collapsed stars. Black holes have such a strong gravitational pull that nothing, not even light, can escape from them, hence their name. The outer boundary of a black hole is known as the event horizon, within which everything is completely cut off from the universe around. However, inside rotating black holes there is a second or inner event horizon, which takes the form of a ring. A spaceship flying into a rotating black hole and entering the ring-shaped inner event horizon would not, it is believed, be crushed to nothing, but would, in theory at least, be instantly regurgitated from a white hole (the two being connected by a 'worm-hole' in space), either in a distant place in this universe (perhaps hundreds of light years from the black hole) or in another universe altogether. Hence teleportation through unimaginable distances could theoretically happen via a black hole.

However, we have seen that teleportation occurs here on earth, if only infrequently. This means that our conventional belief that matter can only move in a linear fashion by using energy to impel it is not the whole truth, even though it describes the vast bulk of physical movements. But just as most distance communication between people is made by letter, telephone or fax, some also takes place by telepathy or direct mind-to-mind contact. A mental/emotional dimension is certainly evident in some cases of teleportation, when acute fear, stress, or anxiety somehow prompts or causes the victim to be instantly removed from the site of danger or distress. Such a crisis affects the conscious mind, which immediately suggests why post-mortem teleportation sometimes happens, as the consciousness, separating from the physical body after death, but perhaps not immediately realizing what has happened to it, may retain sufficient fear or distress to cause the teleportation of its former home.

True supernatural disappearances (as opposed to bodily disintegration) which result in the permanent removal of a person from the world, may be explained by supposing that he or she vanishes by crossing the divide which separates our world from another dimension of being. Such dimensions are worlds like ours (although this may be too narrow a term), wholly material and stable, which either a) occupy the same region of space as we do but are none the less separate from us, or b) are physically remote from us yet are somehow connected with us by 'worm-holes' like those joining a black hole in one universe with a white hole in another. Entry into one or other of these dimensions is provided by a psychic 'doorway', rather like the 'holes' or vacua postulated by Bierce's Dr Hern. Such 'doorways' are not of course permanent structures but can evidently be created, or so it seems, by intense negative emotions, whereby they are summoned into being as safety exits, although certain physical forces like electromagnetism may help them to form. Yet none the less, it seems that sometimes an ordinary and happy person (or even an animal or an object) may accidentally enter such a 'doorway' that has unaccountably opened and mysteriously disappear without trace, in the same way that the inhabitants of other dimensions may sometimes vanish from their worlds and find themselves here.

Yet it is idle to speculate further as we can only guess at the nature of alternative dimensions and of their relationship to ourselves. After all, we know little enough about our own world. The divide which separates them from us is also completely enigmatic, although mystics and other seekers of truth do say that the barrier between ourselves and the higher spiritual realms is completely impenetrable to those whose motives are selfish and materialistic, but as unresistant as gossamer to the pure in heart. It would seem that the barrier between our dimension and any other, as I suggested above, has a similar all-or-nothing quality.

In this regard we should remember the legends found throughout Europe and other parts of the world about the fairies, that strange diminutive folk, like ourselves in many ways but in others so very different. While they are said to frequent out of the way places, they actually come from another realm of being, one that exists within, or is entered via, a hill or the perimeter of a fairy ring. Humans can only enter the fairy world by invitation, by abduction, or by accident. Life there is jolly and pleasant: there is feasting, gaiety, and dancing to wonderful music. Time passes much more slowly than here. Yet going there has its risks, for if the visitor partakes of the fairy food he or she can never return.

We dismiss such tales, as we do those about centaurs, satyrs and nymphs, as being nothing more than the products of human imagination. Yet there are numerous accounts of witnesses which testify to their reality. Hence it seems that their frustrating elusiveness derives from the fact that, knowing as they do how to cross the divide separating their dimension from ours, they are able to vanish from our sight in the twinkling of an eye.

We have become dismissive of mysteries, especially of those which threaten to disturb the house of ordinary, common sense 'scientific' reality that we have comfortably erected around and above us. But just as the Buddha divined through meditation that the material world is nothing more than a sensory illusion, so physics has at last determined that he is right. The only reality is that nothing is as it seems. Indeed, we may say that our entire existence, like the Communist system so eloquently described by Sir Winston Churchill, is a riddle wrapped in a mystery inside an enigma.

And this is why both supernatural disappearances and supernatural appearances are the possible impossible.

Index

Abbas, Abdull Baha, 48
Addison, Joseph, 33
Aglasis (demon), 32
Agreda, 61, 62, 63
Alcmene, 39
    her corpse supernaturally dis-
        appears, 40
Alswanger, Captain, 113–14
Alter ego, *see* Double
Amnesia, 167
Ampharool (genie), 32
Apollonius of Tyana, 21
    teleported to: Ephesus, 22;
        Dicaearchia, 23, 24
Apports, 46
Aptolcater, Master, 31
    his instantaneous travel recipe,
        32
Argonauts, 17, 50
Arimaspi (Scythian tribe), 17
Aristeas, 16
    mysteriously vanishes, 17, 24
Artemon (double of Antiochus II),
    114
Arthur, King, 84
Ashmore, Charles, 138
Astral body, 71, 72, 74
Astypalea, 18, 19
Athamas, 77
Atomic forces, 177
Atomic structure, 176, 177
Avalon, Isle of, 84
Aubrey, John, 25–6, 37
Aulis, 77
Aviragus, King, 83

Banjos, 45
Baring-Gould, Sabine, 99, 100,
    104, 107
Basingwerk Abbey, 37–8
Bathurst, Benjamin, 88
    strange disappearance of, 95–111
Bathurst, Phillida, 101, 102, 110
    strange deaths of her children,
        111
Bede, Venerable, 140–1
Bennett, Arnold, 129
Beswick, Miss, 78
Bierce, Ambrose
    his accounts of supernatural
        disappearances, 130–1,
        134–5, 137–9
    his early life, 132–3
    his own disappearance, 130, 142–3
Bilocation, 11
Birdsong, 37, 175
Black holes, 178
Bozzano, Professor, 165, 166
Broome, Dora, 35
Broomstick, flying on, 32
Buddha, 180
Bulfinch, Thomas, 83
Bull, white, 77
    mysteriously appears, 78
Butcher's boy
    mysteriously vanishes, 85

Caius, Drusus, 20–1, 24, 34
Call, George Cotsford, 99, 108
Camel, Nancy, 84, 85, 86
Chapel of Loretto, 57
Churchill, Sir Winston, 180

Cleomedes, 18
  supernaturally disappears, 19,
    20, 23, 24
Coins, supernatural appearance of,
  45–6
Cottages, the vanishing, 53
Coombs, Farmer William, 79–82
Cows, supernatural movement of,
  78–82
Creighton, Helen, 50
Cristo d'Angelo, 164
Cuccolde, 54
Croydon Hill Devil, 85
Cumpston, Thomas and Annie,
  116–18
Cyzicum, 16, 17
Cyzicus, 17

Dasmarinas, Governor Don
    Gomez, 26
David-Neel, Alexandra, 68, 69
Dawn and her vanishing crew, 147
Day, William Conway, 141–2
de Benavides, Father Alonso, 63,
  64
de Calne, Sir Richard, 43
Delphic oracle, 19
D'Entraiges, Count, 102, 103, 109
d'Esperance, Madame, 121
  her legs disappear, 122–3
Devil-worship, 25, 32, 33
Dibble Bridge, 57
Diderici, 113
  his mysterious disappearance,
    115
Dimensions, other, 40, 45, 93–4,
    109–11, 161, 179–80
Dobunni, Celtic tribe, 84
Domitian, Roman emperor, 22
  his assassination, 23
Double, characteristics of, 59, 60
Durrant, Jean, 125–7
Dwarves, characteristics of, 34

Eclipse, accompanying dis-
    appearances, 14, 24, 116, 175
Ectoplasm, 72
Eglinton, William, 162

Eilean More, 119–20
Eldrige, USS, 150, 151
Electrons, 176, 177
Elia, 173
Elves, characteristics of, 34
Ephesus, 22, 23, 24
Erytheia, 82
Estur, Edward, 115–16
Etruscans, 40
Euphemus, 50

Fairies, abduction by, 35, 36, 180
Fairy-child, 34
Fairy music, 34, 37, 44, 175
Fairy-ring, 34
Familiars, witch's, 32
Flaminius, Caius and his vanishing
    corpse, 20, 23, 39
Flannan Islands, 119
Flight 19, 154
Fort, Charles, 46, 119
Fylgia, 73

Gallatin, 136
Garden, supernatural dis-
    appearance of, 50
Gardner, Gerald, 33
Geddes, Michael, 61, 63
Geller, Uri, 168
  teleportation of, 169–70
Geoffrey of Monmouth, 39
Gervasse of Tilbury, 43–4, 47–8
Gisby, Len and Cynthia, 54–7
Goethe, Wolfgang, 75
Graham, John, 78
Green children, 42–6
Green Meadows of Enchantment,
    49–50
Griffins, 17
Guest-house, supernatural dis-
    appearance of, 51
Guppy, Mrs Samuel, 161–2

Hannibal, 20
Hedges, Mrs Edna, 52–3
Heifer, miraculously appears, 77
Helle, 77
Helsingfors, 121

Heracles, 82
Herodotus, 17, 82
Hermes, 40
Hern, Dr, 129, 179
Hilbert, Nikolaus, 96, 98, 100
Hjelt, Vera, 121, 122, 123
Holinshed, Raphael, 145
Holy Grail, 83, 84
Homer, quoted, 13
Hope, Elizabeth, see d'Esperance
Horses, supernatural movement
    of, 78
Hotel, supernatural disappearance
    of, 56
  opening floor of, 117
Hylaea, 82

Iphigenia, 77
Island Queen, 148–50
Islands of the Blessed, 40

Jewel, Albert J., 153
Joseph of Arimathea, 83
Julius Proculus, 15
Jumano Indians, 61–3

Kalavala, 159
Kessel, Thomas, 167–8
Klitzing, Captain, 97, 100, 101
Knife, teleportation of, 47–8
Krouse, 96, 98, 100

Lang, David, 136
Larch, Oliver, 139
Leamington Spa, 130, 131, 132
Leg bone, supernatural dis-
    appearance of, 50
Lightfoot, Lucy, 116, 128
L'ile a Frisee, 50
Luce e Ombre, 164

Marmara, see Proconnesus
Manila, 27
Mary Celeste, 146–7
Mary of Agreda, the Venerable,
    61–4
Maskell, William, 88
Merlin, 84

Mertens, Christian, 98, 103, 104,
    105
Metapontum, 18
Metella, 77
Mexico City, 26, 27
Mirabelli, Carlo, 163, 164

Nagel, Elizabeth, 98, 100
Napoleon, 97, 113, 115
Neale, Waler, 142
Nebel, Long John, 124
Neff, William, 124–5
Nemesis, 77
Neutrons, 176, 177
Newton, Florence, 25, 33
New York Times, 152, 153
Nordhval, 168

Object-showers, 47
O'Donnell, Elliott, 53, 79
Orpheus, 175
Oxen, white, supernaturally
    appear at Alfriston, 77–8

Pachomius, Abba, 29
  woman appears to, 41–2
Palladius, 29, 30
Palmar, Stuart, 136
Parfitt, Owen, 86–9
Pensionnat de Neuwelcke, 64, 65,
    67
Perez, Gil, 26–7
Perleberg, 95–6, 97
  Bathurst vanishes in, 98–111
Peter Bell, A Tale, 74–5
Philadelphia Experiment, 150–1,
    178
Philostratus, Flavius, 21, 22, 23
Phrixus, 77
Phynnodderee, 36
Pigott-Carleton, Henrietta, double
    of, 73–4
Pole, Wellesley Tudor, 48–9, 75,
    teleportation of, 166–7
Polka dot dress, woman with, 9, 10
Proconnessus, 16
Providence Mark, 148
Psychic doorway, 179

Puharich, Dr Andrija, 168, 169, 170
Pye, Mr and Mrs Clifford, 51
Pythagoras, 18, 21

Quarks, 177
Quirinus, 15, 16

Ralph of Coggeshall, Abbot, 44
Ram, winged, 77
Ring of Travel, 32
Ring, loss and supernatural
      reappearance of, 48–9
Rhayader, 139
Ripperstone Farm, cattle telepor-
      ted from, 79–82
Rodhuish, 85
Romulus, 13
  supernaturally disappears, 14
Rose Marie, 149
Protons, 176

Sagee, Emilie, 65–8
St Alphonsus Liguori, 60
St Andrew, 78, 82
St Anthony of Padua
  teleported, 30–1
  bilocation of, 60
St Columba of Rieti, 31
St Cuthbert, 140–1
St Dunstan, 31
St John of the Cross, 31
St Martin, 43–4
St Peter of Alcantara, 31
Scete, desert of, 29
  young monk of, 30
Schmidt family, 98, 100, 101
Scott, Sir Walter, 113
Scotto, Marquis Carlo Centurione,
    164
  teleportation of, 165–6
Shepton Mallet, 84, 86, 87, 88, 104
Simpson, Geoff and Pauline, 54–7
Sirens, 34
Snook, Susannah, 86
Somerset, 84, 85–6, 89
Soul, 177
Spenser, Edmund, 95

Star Ariel, 156
Star Trek, 178
Star Tiger, 155, 156
Stewart, Donald Ramsay, 141–2
Strode, Henry, 87
Sullivan, Peggy, 70–1
Supernatural disappearances
  types of, 173–4
  factors accompanying, 175

Tabenna, monastery at, 29, 41
Tages, 41
Tagetic doctrine, 41
Tao te Ching, 171
Tarchon, 41
Taurominium, 18
Teleportation, 24, 25, 26, 30, 31,
    33, 37, 45, 48, 49
  of cattle, 78–82, 150, 161, 162,
    163, 165–6, 167, 169, 169–70,
    178
Theodore, 41–2
Thera, volcanic island, 50
Thistlethwayte, Mrs Tryphena,
    102, 104, 105–6
Thomas of Ercildoun ('True
    Thomas'), 36
Thomas, Owen, 139
Thunderstorms, accompanying dis-
    appearances, 14, 24, 84, 90,
    116, 175
Thrasymenus, Lake, 20
Time in fairy world, 35, 36
Tinia, Etruscan god, 41
Translocation, *see* teleportation
Tyana, 21

Vaughan children, the, 159–60
Vesta, 77
Victoria Hotel, 116–18
Viper-woman, 82
Voices, disembodied, 62, 117, 137,
    138–9

Walter of Bierbecke, double of, 74
Wangdu, 69
Weichselmunde fortress, 115

Wellington (retriever dog), 169
White Swan Inn, 97–108
Wight, Isle of, 116
Wilkins, Harold T., 159, 169
William of Newburgh, 42
Williamson, 'Orion', 135
Williamson, Peter,
   vanishes, 90
   reappears, 90, 91–4
Wolmar, 65
Woolpit, Suffolk, 43

green children at, 43–5
Worson, James Burne, 130–1

Yorkshire terrier, supernaturally
   disappears, 9, 10
Ynys-witrin, 83

Zeus, 40
   transforms himself into white
   bull, 77
   into white swan, 77, 94